Clipper™
dBASE®

Compiler
Applications

Gary Beam

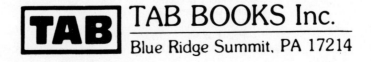

TAB BOOKS Inc.

Blue Ridge Summit, PA 17214

Clipper: dBASE Compiler Applications is dedicated to my parents for their years of support, and to Julie for her continual encouragement.

FIRST EDITION
FIRST PRINTING

Copyright © 1987 by TAB BOOKS Inc.
Printed in the United States of America

Library of Congress Cataloging in Publication Data

Beam, Gary.
Clipper, dBASE compiler applications.

Includes index.
1. Compilers (Computer programs) 2. Clipper
(Computer program) 3. dBASE III (Computer program)
I. Title.
QA76.76.C65B43   1987   005.4'53   87-7128
ISBN 0-8306-2917-3 (pbk.)

Questions regarding the content of this book
should be addressed to:

Reader Inquiry Branch
Editorial Department
TAB BOOKS Inc.
P.O. Box 40
Blue Ridge Summit, PA 17214

Contents

Introduction

Consider the typical dBASE III PLUS application program. It is distributed on one or more diskettes along with associated database files. It can only be used on computers that already have dBASE III PLUS installed. It cannot run at optimum computer speed, because the program must operate with the dBASE interpreter. The source code is not protected.

Now consider what compiling a dBASE application offers. It can often be distributed as a single program on a single diskette, because the database files can be created from within the program. It requires no additional software other than DOS. It requires no interpreter and therefore runs at computer speed, often 10 times faster than dBASE. Compiled source code is nearly impossible to decode, thereby offering built-in protection to the programmer.

The Clipper compiler from Nantucket provides many significant enhancements to the dBASE language. There are additional commands that the dBASE programmer can utilize in application software development. Clipper compiling also allows the programmer to incorporate libraries of custom-designed dBASE-like functions.

This book is written for users of the Nantucket Clipper compiler. It is not a book of theory, but rather a book of methods and techniques. The beginning user of Clipper will benefit from the programming examples, which go beyond Nantucket's user manual. The experienced Clipper user will find alternate programming methods or styles that will enhance programming proficiency.

Clipper: dBASE Compiler Applications utilizes a do-by-example approach. A typical Sales Management Information System (SMIS) application is used as the real-world programming example throughout the book. This system is designed to track customers, salespersons, basic inventory, and customer orders. SMIS is self-installing, menu driven, and password protected; it even includes a built-in user help facility. The program uses methods, commands, and functions that are only available with Clipper.

The discussion begins in Chapter 1 with a review of proper program structure. Tips on organizing and naming program files are presented. The program, database, and index structure for the Sales Management Information System example are explained. The complete source code for this SMIS application example is included in Appendix A.

Chapter 2 discusses program initialization techniques, including a multilevel password entry scheme, and the creation of database files from within an application.

Chapter 3 presents two methods for generating light-bar menus. The first method is compatible with dBASE; the second is for Clipper users only.

Data entry and change techniques are demonstrated in Chapters 4 and 5. Clipper methods of data validation are explained in detail.

Data list and data print routines are discussed in Chapter 6. Included are ways to scroll a database forward or backward and to print formal reports.

Chapter 7 shows how to perform data backup operations from within an application.

Chapter 8 offers an in-depth discussion of the Clipper Help function. Help can be accessed from any point in a Clipper-compiled application, including menus. A complete user manual can be built into an application via the Help function.

Chapter 9 discusses user-defined functions and how to make use of them in any application.

Compiling and linking examples are presented in Chapters 10 and 11.

Appendix A contains the complete source code for the Sales Management Information System application example used throughout the book.

Appendix B contains the source code for dFILER, a programmer's utility that contains several interactive database commands that will be useful to the Clipper user.

Appendix C consists of a summary of Clipper commands used in the book, and Appendix D consists of a summary of Clipper functions used in the book.

Author's Note

Experienced users of the Nantucket Clipper compiler are aware of the differences that unfortunately exist between dBASE and Clipper. There are commands in dBASE that might not be compatible with Clipper, and vice versa. An application written in dBASE might not compile unless these differences are accommodated.

Fortunately, Nantucket has provided a special variable, interestingly enough called *Clipper,* that can be used to handle the few language differences.

Normally, at the start-up of a dBASE or Clipper program, all memory variables are initialized as a logical false (.F.). In a Clipper compiled program, however, the special variable Clipper is initialized as a logical true (.T.). By using this variable properly, a single application can be developed that will operate either compiled with Clipper or executed under dBASE, even though the command syntax might vary between the two.

For example, the dBASE instructions for drawing a box on the screen do not recognize the Clipper BOX command. Using BOX in a dBASE program will cause it to crash. Using the dBASE box syntax in a Clipper application will likewise interrupt operation. The Clipper memory variable takes care of the difference.

```
PUBLIC Clipper
PUBLIC mFRAME1
mFRAME1 = CHR(218)+CHR(196)+CHR(191)+CHR(179)+;
    CHR(217)+CHR(196)+CHR(192)+CHR(179)
IF .NOT. Clipper
   @ 5,10 TO 10,70
ELSE
   @ 5,10,10,70 BOX mFRAME1
ENDIF
```

Note, in the code shown, that the memvar Clipper and the necessary BOX description, mFRAME1, were declared PUBLIC, so that they can be used throughout an application.

It must be noted that using the Clipper memvar might result in errors being displayed during compiling. For example, the dBASE instructions for drawing the box will result in an error notation during Clipper compiling, but the program will still compile, link, and run successfully.

The programs in this book are based on the Winter 1985 release from Nantucket. This includes libraries dated 01/29/86 and 05/30/86. References to dBASE throughout the book refer to dBASE III PLUS from Ashton-Tate.

Chapter 1

Program Structure

A vital task in the development of any application is the structuring of the programs. Although this is largely a matter of style, the techniques used here have proven to be most effective in creating an orderly program structure.

PROGRAM NAMES

Program names in *Clipper: dBASE Compiler Applications* start with a letter followed by an underscore. The first letter signifies the type of activity the program performs, such as m__ for a menu program, e__ for a data-entry program, and so on.

Both dBASE and Clipper allow programs to call other programs and even to pass parameters between them. This means that regularly used routines can be placed in a separate program and called up when needed, thus reducing overall code size. Ideal examples of called routines include error routines and warning messages. Programs of this type are considered utility programs in this book, and are named u__.

Appendix A includes the source code for the Sales Management Information System (SMIS). This code incorporates all of the techniques discussed in *Clipper: dBASE Compiler Applications*.

```
smis            Initialization, Logo & Password Entry
m_main          Main Menu
  m_cust        Customer Menu
    e_cust      Enter a customer
    c_cust      Change/Delete a customer
    l_cust      List customers
  m_ordr        Sales Orders Menu
    e_ordr      Enter a sales order
    c_ordr      Change/Delete a sales order
    l_ordr      List/Print sales orders
  m_inve        Inventory Menu
    e_inve      Enter an inventory item
    c_inve      Change/Delete an inventory item
    l_inve      List/Print inventory
  m_sale        Salesman Menu
    e_sale      Enter a salesperson
    c_sale      Change/Delete a salesperson
    l_sale      List/Print salespersons
  m_pass        Password Menu
    e_pass      Enter a password
    c_pass      Change a password
    l_pass      List/Print passwords
  m_data        Data Backup Menu
    b_data      Backup data to floppy
    r_data      Recall backed up data
    i_data      Index databases
help            User-help
  h_main        Main Menu Help
  h_cust        Customer Menu Help
  h_ordr        Sales Order Menu Help
  h_inve        Inventory Menu Help
  h_sale        Salesperson Menu Help
  h_pass        Password Menu Help
  h_data        Data Backup Menu Help
u_entr          Data entry utility
u_chng          Data change utility
u_upda          Data update utility
u_list          Data list utility
u_sure          Are you sure (delete) utility
u_nofi          Not found utility
u_infi          Already in file utility
u_deny          Access Denied utility
```

Fig. 1-1. The programs in the SMIS example.

PROGRAM STRUCTURE

Forty-two separate modules (programs) are used to perform the SMIS functions. The individual programs, which are listed in Fig. 1-1, can be compiled to create a single SMIS.EXE file.

A block diagram is often useful in defining the program structure. A diagram for the SMIS example application is shown in Fig. 1-2.

DATABASE STRUCTURE

As shown in Table 1-1, the SMIS example uses five database

files to store the entered information. Some of these files will become related during many of the programs, thereby eliminating the need to duplicate fields from one database to another. For example, the cost of an item is available to the orders database (ORDR.DBF) by setting a relationship with the inventory database (INVE.DBF). Their common field is the item number (ITEMNR) field (see Fig. 1-3.)

INDEX STRUCTURE

Fig. 1-2. Program structure diagram.

As shown in Table 1-2, each SMIS database file has one associated index file. The index file maintains the proper sequence of database records without having to continually sort the database.

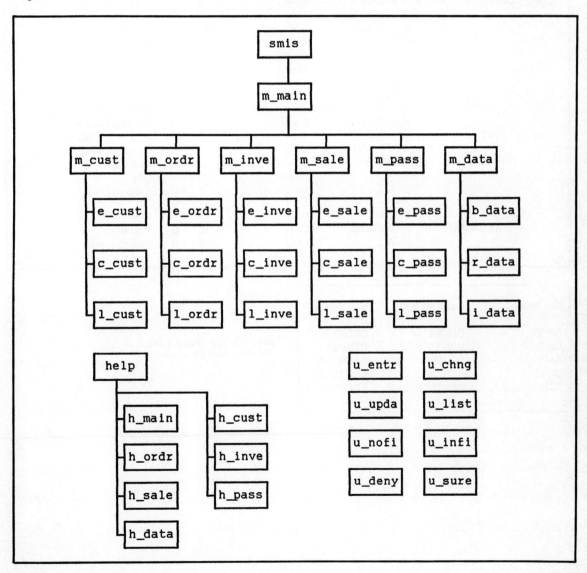

Table 1-1. The Five Database Files Used in the SMIS Example.

File Name	Field Name	Type	Width	Dec	Description
ORDR	ORDRNR	Char	3	0	Order Number
	CUSTCODE	Char	3	0	Customer Code
	SALECODE	Char	3	0	Salesman Code
	QTY	Num	4	0	Quantity
	ITEMNR	Char	3	0	Item Number
	DATE	Date	8	0	Order Date
INVE	ITEMNR	Char	3	0	Item Number
	DESC	Char	20	0	Description
	COST	Num	8	2	Item Cost
SALE	SALECODE	Char	3	0	Salesman Code
	SALENAME	Char	20	0	Salesman Name
	ADDRESS	Char	20	0	Address
	CITY	Char	20	0	City
	STATE	Char	2	0	State
	ZIP	Char	5	0	Zip Code
	PHONE	Char	10	0	Phone Number
	AGE	Num	2	0	Age
	HIRED	Date	8	0	Date Hired
	BASEPAY	Num	6	2	Monthly Base Pay
CUST	CUSTCODE	Char	3	0	Customer Code
	CUSTNAME	Char	20	0	Customer Name
	ADDRESS	Char	20	0	Address
	CITY	Char	20	0	City
	STATE	Char	2	0	State
	ZIP	Char	5	0	Zip
	PHONE	Char	12	0	Phone
PASSWORD	PASSWORD	Char	10	0	Password
	LEVEL	Char	1	0	Security Level

File Name	Index Name	Key Fields
ORDR	ORDR1	ORDRNR
INVE	INVE1	ITEMNR
SALE	SALE1	SALECODE
CUST	CUST1	CUSTCODE
PASSWORD	PASSWORD	PASSWORD

Table 1-2. The Index Files for the SMIS Example.

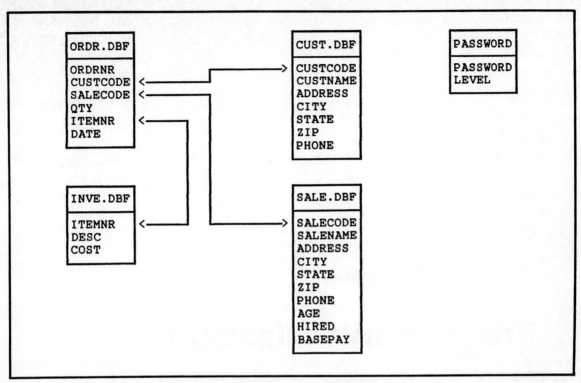

Fig. 1-3. Database structure diagram.

Chapter 2

Program Initialization

The first operating section of any application should set up the operating environment for the rest of the program. This chapter describes how to initialize parameters and variables, create database files from within an application program, and develop a password security system.

INITIALIZATION

Certain parameters must be initialized through dBASE and Clipper SET commands. Some of these retain the same status throughout a program; others may be changed when necessary.

The first SMIS program (smis.prg) sets four parameters and initializes four variables:

```
* Program .......... smis.prg
* Description ...... Initialization Program
SET CONFIRM ON
SET BELL OFF
SET DELETED ON
SET ESCAPE OFF
```

The SET CONFIRM ON command requires that the user press the Enter key to complete entry of any data item. With the alternative, SET CONFIRM OFF, data entry is automatically completed when the end of the field is reached.

The computer bell (or beep) can be suppressed during program operation by using the SET BELL OFF command. Various SMIS operations use the computer bell to indicate a warning or error. In these special instances, the bell may be sounded with a ? CHR(7) command.

Deleted records will be displayed during listing activities unless they are turned off with SET DELETED OFF. Records in the SMIS example are never PACKED; therefore any deleted records must be suppressed.

The Esc (Escape) key can be used to stop a running Clipper program unless turned off with SET ESCAPE OFF. Additionally, if not turned off, the Esc key can be used during data entry to exit data GET statements.

In order for a variable to be used throughout a program, it must be declared public. A variable that is not declared public will be recognized only by the program in which it is used, or by lower-level programs that are called by that program.

Memory variables, whether public or private, are also referred to as *memvars*. Throughout the program in this book, memvars are denoted by the m prefix. This is done in order to avoid confusion between memvars and their database field equivalents. For example, mORDRNR is the memvar equivalent of the database field ORDRNR. Here are some of the PUBLIC declarations used in SMIS:

```
PUBLIC mPW          && the user-entered password
PUBLIC mAL          && the access level (per password)
PUBLIC mCHOICE      && used in some utility routines
PUBLIC mFRAME1      && used in Clipper single-boxes
PUBLIC mSURE        && delete verify variable
```

Some public variables should be defined during the initialization of the program, such as the mFRAME1 dimension (shown below) used in creating windows (boxes) on the screen with the Clipper BOX command.

```
mFRAME1 = CHR(218)+CHR(196)+CHR(191)+CHR(179)+;
CHR(217)+CHR(196)+CHR(192)+CHR(179)
```

The initialization program may include an introductory screen for the user. This usually includes the program name (or logo) and the copyright notice.

The initial screen in the sales management program uses a logo consisting of the acronym SMIS along with the complete title and copyright notice (see Fig. 2-1). The introduction is displayed for five

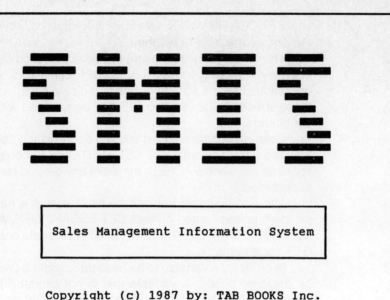

```
          ┌────────────────────────────────────────────────┐
          │                                                │
          │   ███  █   █  ████  ███                        │
          │   ███  █   █  ████  ███    (SMIS logo)         │
          │                                                │
          │  ┌──────────────────────────────────────────┐  │
          │  │  Sales Management Information System      │  │
          │  └──────────────────────────────────────────┘  │
          │                                                │
          │   Copyright (c) 1987 by: TAB BOOKS Inc.        │
          │  ─────────────────────────────────────────     │
          │                                                │
          └────────────────────────────────────────────────┘
```

Sales Management Information System

seconds, the screen is cleared, and a permanent screen heading is displayed.

Fig. 2-1. The initialization screen.

The Clipper INKEY( ) function produces the five second interval, which may be shortened by a user keypress. The number enclosed in parentheses is equal to the number of delay seconds. This time is "real" time, and is not related to the computer operating speed.

As shown below, the code for displaying the SMIS logo uses an x to represent the graphic character used in the logo display. This character may be typed in directly on an IBM-type keyboard by pressing and holding the Alt key while entering 2 2 0 on the keypad for each x.

```
    CLEAR
    SET COLOR TO W+
    @ 3,20 SAY " xxxxx     xxxx    xxxx   xxxxxxx     xxxxx        "
    @ 4,20 SAY "xxxxxxx    xxxx    xxxx   xxxxxxx    xxxxxxx       "
    @ 5,20 SAY "xxx        xxxxx  xxxxx     xxx        xxx         "
    @ 6,20 SAY " xxx        xxxxxxxxxxx     xxx        xxx         "
    @ 7,20 SAY "  xxx       xxx xxx xxx     xxx        xxx         "
    @ 8,20 SAY "   xxx      xxx  x  xxx     xxx         xxx        "
    @ 9,20 SAY "    xxx     xxx     xxx     xxx         xxx        "
    @10,20 SAY "xxxxxxx     xxx     xxx   xxxxxxx     xxxxxxx       "
    @11,20 SAY " xxxxx      xxx     xxx   xxxxxxx      xxxxx        "
    @15,20,19,60 SAY BOX mFRAME1"
    SET COLOR TO W
    @17,23 SAY "Sales Management Information System"
```

```
SET COLOR TO W+
@22,22 SAY "Copyright (c) 1987 by: TAB BOOKS Inc."
SET COLOR TO W
@23,22 SAY REPLICATE(CHR(196),37)
? INKEY(5) && a five-second time delay
CLEAR
```

A screen title for each activity in the Sales Management Information System will appear on line three of the permanent heading. This heading is never erased during program operation (see Fig. 2-2).

```
@ 1,20,4,60 BOX mFRAME1
@ 2,23 SAY "Sales Management Information System"
```

INSTALLATION

In many Clipper-compiled applications, the programmer must supply the user with not only the executable (.EXE) program, but also the associated database (.DBF) files. Clipper includes the commands that are required to create database files from within any application program. This means that the distribution diskette for a program need only contain the program itself.

The first step in creating a database is to define field names, types, and lengths (including the number of places after the decimal if the field is numeric). This information is then appended to a dummy file in *structure-extended format*, that is, to a database with

Fig. 2-2. The installation screen.

```
┌─────────────────────────────────────────────────────┐
│  ┌───────────────────────────────────────────────┐  │
│  │   Sales  Management  Information  System       │  │
│  │               INSTALLATION                     │  │
│  └───────────────────────────────────────────────┘  │
│                                                      │
│                                                      │
│        ORDR.DBF  is  created  and  indexed           │
│                                                      │
│                                                      │
│                                                      │
│                                                      │
│                                                      │
│                                                      │
└─────────────────────────────────────────────────────┘
```

a structure containing the field data.

Field Name	Type	Length	Decimal
FIELDNAME	Char	10	0
FIELDTYPE	Char	1	0
FIELDLEN	Num	3	0
FIELDDEC	Num	1	0
		15	

Once the field names are defined and appended to DUMMY.DBF, the Clipper CREATE FROM command is used to create the final database with a structure as defined in DUMMY.

In the SMIS example, one of the required database files is called ORDR. The initialization program (see the code segment shown below) first checks for the existence of the database. If the file already exists, then no installation is required. If the file does not exist, then the activity name (INSTALLATION) is displayed in the screen heading and the database files are created.

The exclamation sign (!) in Clipper is equivalent to the .NOT. operator. For example, IF .NOT. FOUND( ) may also be expressed as IF ! FOUND( ). The FILE function returns a logical false (.F.) if the database file ORDR does not exist.

Note that in Clipper, comments may be added at the end of a program line by using a double ampersand (&&) separator.

```
IF ! FILE("ORDR.DBF")   && the ! is the same as .NOT.
   SET COLOR TO W+
      @ 3,25 SAY SPACE(30)
      @ 3,34 SAY "INSTALLATION"
   SET COLOR TO W
   CREATE DUMMY && the dummy structure-extended file
   STORE "ORDRNR    C3 " TO Field1
   STORE "CUSTCODE  C3 " TO Field2
   STORE "SALECODE  C3 " TO Field3
   STORE "QTY       N4 " TO Field4
   STORE "ITEMNR    C3 " TO Field5
   STORE "DATE      D5 " TO Field6
```

A loop is set up to append the field information to the file DUMMY. Clipper allows use of the FOR. . .NEXT command, much like that used in BASIC programming. Note that a macro designated by an ampersand (&) prefix must be used to name the field variable number (FN):

```
FOR F = 1 TO 6              && since there are 6 fields
   IF F < 10                && could have over 10 fields
      STORE STR(F,1) TO count
```

```
        ELSE
              STORE STR(F,2) TO count
        ENDIF
        APPEND BLANK
        STORE "Field" + count TO FN $
        REPLACE field_name WITH SUBSTR(&FN,1,10)
        REPLACE field_type WITH SUBSTR(&FN,11,1)
        REPLACE field_len WITH VAL(SUBSTR(&FN,12,2))
        REPLACE field_dec WITH VAL(SUBSTR(&FN,14,1))
        F=F+1
   NEXT
```

Next, the file ORDR.DBF can be created from the structure-extended DUMMY file and also may be indexed as required:

```
     CREATE ORDR FROM DUMMY
     INDEX ON ORDRNR TO ORDR1
     CLOSE DATABASES
   ENDIF
```

A message can be displayed to the user to indicate the status of the installation process:

```
@11,25 SAY "ORDR.DBF is created and indexed"
```

The dummy database DUMMY.DBF can be erased, because it is no longer needed:

```
ERASE DUMMY.DBF
```

The remaining databases are created in a similar manner, as shown in the complete source code in Appendix A.

PASSWORD ENTRY

A password security system is often required in applications programming. The user is prompted to enter an exact password before being allowed to continue. In some applications, it is desirable to use more than one password and assign an access level to each password. The access level controls which activities are available to the user who entered the password (see Fig. 2-3).

The SMIS example includes a database called PASSWORD, which contains a password and access-level code. The user is allowed to enter, change, and delete passwords and codes as

```
┌─────────────────────────────────────────────────────────────┐
│                                                             │
│        ┌──────────────────────────────────────────┐        │
│        │  Sales Management Information System      │        │
│        │         PASSWORD ENTRY                    │        │
│        └──────────────────────────────────────────┘        │
│                                                             │
│                                                             │
│                                                             │
│               Enter your password ....                      │
│                                                             │
│                                                             │
│                                                             │
│                                                             │
│                                                             │
│                                                             │
└─────────────────────────────────────────────────────────────┘
```

necessary. The code for password entry is shown below:

Fig. 2-3. The password entry screen.

```
DO WHILE .T.
    SET COLOR TO W+
        @ 3,25 SAY SPACE(30)
        @ 3,33 SAY "PASSWORD ENTRY"
    SET COLOR TO W
    STORE SPACE(10) TO mPW
    STORE SPACE(1) TO mAL
    SET COLOR TO W+
        @12,28 SAY "Enter your password .... "
    SET COLOR TO W
    SET CONSOLE OFF
    ACCEPT TO mPW
    SET CONSOLE ON
```

The entered password must be tested for a blank entry. The Clipper EMPTY function tests any type of variable (Character, Date, Logical, or Numeric) for a blank entry. If the entered password is blank, the password loop restarts.

```
IF EMPTY(mPW)
    LOOP
ENDIF
```

The entered password must first be converted to uppercase, since the database file PASSWORD.DBF contains only uppercase data. PASSWORD.DBF is then checked to see if the entered password exists in the file. SET EXACT ON is used to ensure an exact password match.

If the entered password is not found in the file, the program loops back to the beginning for another entry attempt. If the password is found, the access level is stored in the PUBLIC memvar mAL and the program continues to the Main Menu:

```
STORE UPPER(mPW) TO mPW
USE PASSWORD INDEX PASSWORD
SET EXACT ON
FIND "&mPW"
IF ! FOUND( )
    SET EXACT OFF
    USE
    LOOP
ELSE
    STORE LEVEL TO mAL
    SET EXACT OFF
    USE
    DO m_main
  ENDIF
ENDDO
* End of smis.prg
```

Chapter 3

Menu Programs

All menus created by the programs discussed here utilize the light-bar technique. The menu is scrolled by using the cursor keys. Menu choices appear in reverse video as they are scrolled. This creates the same menu appearance as some of the top-selling commercial software programs.

A choice is selected by pressing the Enter key when the desired choice is highlighted. Alternatively, a choice may be selected by pressing the first letter in the name of any choice.

Two different main menu examples for the SMIS example program are included in this discussion. Both provide exactly the same menu appearance.

The dBASE MENU

The dBASE version of the main menu program (m__main.prg), which also works with Clipper, is built around the INKEY() function. The menu is displayed, and the program waits for an acceptable user keypress. Once the Enter key or a key corresponding to the first letter of a choice is pressed, the program continues to the next menu or activity.

The SMIS main menu consists of eight choices, each having a brief message of explanation (see Fig. 3-1). These are defined at the beginning of the program.

```
┌─────────────────────────────────────────────────────────┐
│      ┌──────────────────────────────────────────┐       │
│      │  Sales Management Information System      │       │
│      │              MAIN MENU                    │       │
│      └──────────────────────────────────────────┘       │
│                                                         │
│                                                         │
│                                                         │
│                 Customers                               │
│                 Orders                                  │
│                 Inventory                               │
│                 Salespersons                            │
│                 Passwords                               │
│                 Backup                                  │
│                 Return                                  │
│                 Quit                                    │
│                                                         │
│                                                         │
│                                                         │
│                                                         │
│                                                         │
│                                                         │
│      Enter, change, or list Customer Information        │
│                                                         │
│                                                         │
└─────────────────────────────────────────────────────────┘
```

Fig. 3-1. The main menu screen.

The menu choices are labelled C1 through C8, and the corresponding messages are labelled M1 through M8:

```
* Program . . . . . . . . . m_main (dBASE and Clipper)
* Description . . . . . . Main Menu
DO WHILE .T.
      SET COLOR TO W+
         @ 5,0 CLEAR
         @ 3,25 SAY SPACE(30)
         @ 3,36 SAY "MAIN MENU"
      SET COLOR TO W
      C1 = "Customers"
      C2 = "Orders"
      C3 = "Inventory"
      C4 = "Salespersons"
      C5 = "Passwords"
      C6 = "Backup"
      C7 = "Return"
      C8 = "Quit"
      M1 = "Enter, change, or list Customer Information"
      M2 = "  Enter, change, or list Customer Orders"
      M3 = "       Enter, change, or list Inventory"
      M4 = "    Enter, change, or list Salespersons"
      M5 = "     Enter, change, or list Passwords"
      M6 = "         Backup or Recall floppy data"
      M7 = "              Return to Password"
      M8 = "                 Quit to DOS"
```

The total number of choices (quan) and the value of the starting menu memvar (main) must be initialized as shown below.

```
quan = 8
main = 1
```

The choices are initially displayed in normal video and centered on the screen, using the following commands.

```
@  8,34 SAY C1
@  9,34 SAY C2
@10,34 SAY C3
@11,34 SAY C4
@12,34 SAY C5
@13,34 SAY C6
@14,34 SAY C7
@15,34 SAY C8
```

The DO WHILE command is used to display the current choice in reverse video (see the code segment shown below)and the corresponding message in normal video. The current-choice memvar (CX) consists of "C" plus the value of the menu memvar (main). The current-message memvar (MX) consists of "M" plus the value of the menu memvar (main). Both CX and MX are character memvars, and must be called by using the macro substitution function(&).

```
DO WHILE .T.
    CX = "C" + STR(main,1)
    MX = "M" + STR(main,1)
    SET COLOR TO /W
        @ 7+main,26 SAY &CX
    SET COLOR TO W
        @22,19 SAY &MX
```

Yet another DO WHILE command loop is used to await the user keypress, which may be the up-arrow key, the down-arrow key, the Enter key, or a key corresponding to the first letter in a choice name. Once the keypress has occurred, each of these conditions must be tested checked for.

If the keypress was the Enter key or a first letter key, the loop is exited, because the user has made a selection. If the up-arrow or down-arrow key was pressed, the menu memvar is incremented or decremented accordingly:

```
key = 0
    DO WHILE key = 0
        key = INKEY( )
```

```
                ENDDO
                IF key = 13 && Was Enter key (13) pressed?
                    EXIT
                ENDIF
                IF key = 5 && Was up arrow key (5) pressed?
                    main = main - 1
                    IF main < 1
                        main = quan
                    ENDIF
                ENDIF
                IF key = 24 && Was down arrow key (24) pressed?
                    main = main + 1
                    IF main > quan
                        main = 1
                    ENDIF
                ENDIF
                IF UPPER(CHR(key)) = "C" && Was C key pressed?
                    main = 1
                    EXIT
                ENDIF
                IF UPPER(CHR(key)) = "O" && Was O key pressed?
                    main = 2
                    EXIT
                ENDIF
                IF UPPER(CHR(key)) = "I" && Was I key pressed?
                    main = 3
                    EXIT
                ENDIF
                IF UPPER(CHR(key)) = "S" && Was S key pressed?
                    main = 4
                    EXIT
                ENDIF
                IF UPPER(CHR(key)) = "P" && Was P key pressed?
                    main = 5
                    EXIT
                ENDIF
                IF UPPER(CHR(key)) = "B" && Was B key pressed?
                    main = 6
                    EXIT
                ENDIF
                IF UPPER(CHR(key)) = "R" && Was R key pressed?
                    main = 7
                    EXIT
                ENDIF
                IF UPPER(CHR(key)) = "Q" && Was Q key pressed?
                    main = 8
                    EXIT
                ENDIF
                LOOP
        ENDDO
```

The DO CASE command is used to decide which action to take once the user has made a selection, as shown, below. Choices 1 through 6 allow the user to continue to the appropriate submenu. Choice 7 causes a return to Password Entry in the calling program (smis.prg). Choice 8 causes a termination of the SMIS program and a return to DOS through the use of the QUIT command.

```
        DO CASE
            CASE main = 1
                DO m__cust
            CASE main = 2
                DO m__ordr
            CASE main = 3
                DO m__inve
            CASE main = 4
                DO m__sale
            CASE main = 5
                DO m__pass
            CASE main = 6
                DO m__back
            CASE main = 7
                EXIT
            CASE main = 8
                CLEAR
                QUIT
        ENDCASE
    ENDDO
    RELEASE ALL
    RETURN
    * End of m__main
```

THE CLIPPER MENU

The Clipper version of the main menu is unique because it utilizes Clipper's MENU TO, PROMPT, and SET MESSAGE commands. The HELP function is also available in the Clipper version; it is discussed in detail in Chapter 8. The Clipper version takes far less code to produce the same menu.

Menu selections are displayed using the Clipper PROMPT command, and corresponding messages are displayed using the SET MESSAGE command. The choice memvar (main) starts with a value of one. Line 22 is used for messages, and must be indicated by the SET MESSAGE TO command:

```
    * Program . . . . . . . . . m__main (Clipper only)
    * Description . . . . . . Main Menu
    DO WHILE .T.
        main = 1
        SET MESSAGE TO 22
        @ 8,35 PROMPT "Customers"          MESSAGE SPACE(19)+;
            " Enter, change, or list Customer Information "
```

18

```
@ 9,35 PROMPT "Orders"          MESSAGE SPACE(19) + ;
        " Enter, change, or list Customer Orders "
@10,35 PROMPT "Inventory"       MESSAGE SPACE(19) + ;
        " Enter, change, or list Inventory "
@11,35 PROMPT "Salespersons"    MESSAGE SPACE(19) + ;
        " Enter, change, or list Salespersons "
@12,35 PROMPT "Passwords"       MESSAGE SPACE(19) + ;
        " Enter, change, or list Passwords "
@13,35 PROMPT "Backup"          MESSAGE SPACE(19) + ;
        " Backup or Recall from floppy "
@14,35 PROMPT "Return"          MESSAGE SPACE(19) + ;
        " Return to password entry "
@15,35 PROMPT "Quit"            MESSAGE SPACE(19) + ;
        " Quit to DOS. "
```

The Clipper **MENU TO** command is used to read the user keypress. Automatically, it looks for the up-arrow, down-arrow, Enter, first letter, or F1 key.

```
MENU TO main
```

As in the INKEY example, the DO CASE command is used to decide which activity to perform next using the following sequence of commands.

```
DO CASE
    CASE main = 1
        DO m__cust
    CASE main = 2
        DO m__ordr
    CASE main = 3
        DO m__inve
    CASE main = 4
        DO m__sale
    CASE main = 5
        DO m__pass
    CASE main = 6
        DO m__back
    CASE main = 7
        EXIT
    CASE main = 8
        CLEAR
        QUIT
    ENDCASE
ENDDO
RELEASE ALL
@ 5,0 CLEAR
RETURN
* End of m__main (Clipper)
```

A CLIPPER SUBMENU

Sometimes, it is desirable to have a submenu appear on the screen after a primary menu selection has been made. An example of this appears in the Orders menu in the Sales Management application (see Fig. 3-2). This menu has four primary choices: enter, change, list, and return. If the user selects the list option, a submenu is displayed in a window (box) below the primary menu with a line connecting the box to the list choice. This submenu gives the user choices about the way in which the orders information is listed. The user may list all orders, or list them per customer, per item, or per salesperson. Again, the user scrolls through the submenu with the cursor keys and selects an option with the Enter key or the first letter of a name.

Help is also accessible from the submenu, (discussed in Chapter 8). For that reason, two different choice memvars must be used in this menu, as shown below. Initially, the primary choice memvar (ordr1) is set to 1, but the submenu choice memvar (ordr2) must be set to 9.

```
* Program . . . . . . . . . . m_ordr
* Description . . . . . . Orders Menu
DO WHILE .T.
     SET COLOR TO W+
        @ 5,0 CLEAR
        @ 3,25 SAY SPACE(30)
```

Fig. 3-2. The orders menu screen.

```
+------------------------------------------------------+
|                                                      |
|     +----------------------------------------+       |
|     |  Sales Management Information System    |       |
|     |            ORDERS MENU                  |       |
|     +----------------------------------------+       |
|                                                      |
|                                                      |
|                                                      |
|                    Enter                             |
|                    Change                            |
|                    List                              |
|                    Return                            |
|                                                      |
|                                                      |
|                                                      |
|                                                      |
|            Enter a new order                         |
|                                                      |
+------------------------------------------------------+
```

```
                    @ 3,35 SAY "ORDERS MENU"
            SET COLOR TO W
            ordr1 = 1
            ordr2 = 9
            SET MESSAGE TO 22
            @ 8,37 PROMPT "Enter"              MESSAGE SPACE(28) + ;
              " Enter a new order. "
            @ 9,37 PROMPT "Change"             MESSAGE SPACE(28) + ;
              " Change or delete an order. "
            @10,37 PROMPT "List"               MESSAGE SPACE(28) + ;
              " List sales orders. "
            @11,37 PROMPT "Return"             MESSAGE SPACE(28) + ;
              " To return to the Main Menu. "
            MENU TO ordr1
```

As in the main menu, the DO CASE command determines which activity comes next (see the code shown below). If "list" is selected, the submenu is displayed. Note that at the start of the submenu, the submenu choice memvar (ordr2) is reset to 1.

```
            DO CASE
                CASE ordr1 = 1
                    DO e_ordr
                CASE ordr1 = 2
                    DO c_ordr
                CASE ordr1 = 3
                    ordr2 = 1
```

The sub-menu window is displayed with a connecting line from the list choice to the window (see Fig. 3-3). Note that additional messages for the submenu are also displayed in this example:

```
@10,41 SAY REPLICATE(CHR(196),5)
@10,46 SAY CHR(191)
@11,46 SAY CHR(179)
@12,46 SAY CHR(179)
@13,42,19,61 BOX mFRAME1
@13,46 SAY CHR(193)
@14,43 PROMPT "All Orders ";
    MESSAGE SPACE(17) + ;
    " To list all orders "
@15,43 PROMPT "Customer Select ";
    MESSAGE SPACE(17) + ;
    "To only list orders per a selected customer "
@16,43 PROMPT "Item Select ";
    MESSAGE SPACE(17) + ;
    "To only list orders per a selected item "
@17,43 PROMPT "Salesperson Select";
    MESSAGE SPACE(17) + ;
    "To only list orders per a selected salesperson"
```

```
┌──────────────────────────────────────────────────────────────────────┐
│                                                                        │
│              ┌────────────────────────────────────────┐                │
│              │  Sales Management Information System     │                │
│              │             ORDERS MENU                  │                │
│              └────────────────────────────────────────┘                │
│                                                                        │
│                                                                        │
│                                 Enter                                  │
│                                 Change                                 │
│                                 List──────┐                            │
│                                 Return    │                            │
│                                           │                            │
│                                  ┌────────┴──────────────┐             │
│                                  │  All Orders           │             │
│                                  │  Customer Select      │             │
│                                  │  Item Number Select   │             │
│                                  │  Salesperson Select   │             │
│                                  │  Return               │             │
│                                  └───────────────────────┘             │
│                                                                        │
│                                                                        │
│                      To list all orders                                │
│                                                                        │
└──────────────────────────────────────────────────────────────────────┘
```

@18,43 PROMPT "Return";
    MESSAGE SPACE(17)+;
    " Return to the primary menu "
MENU TO ordr2

Fig. 3-3. The orders submenu screen.

A single program (l_ordr.prg) is used to list customer orders. The choice memvar (ordr2) is passed as a parameter to that program so that the selected listing conditions can be set as shown below. The choice is first tested for a return to the primary menu.

```
            IF ordr2 = 5
                LOOP
            ELSE
                DO l_ordr WITH ordr2
            ENDIF
            CASE ordr1 = 4
                EXIT
        ENDCASE
ENDDO
RELEASE ALL
RETURN
* End of m_ordr.prg
```

Chapter 4

Data Entry Programs

Data entry must be treated as a highly critical activity in any program application. Improper data entry can lead to corrupted data files or even data loss. This chapter discusses techniques that lead to error-free data entry and thus, data file integrity.

SEQUENCE

Two very important factors in this discussion are *memory variables* (memvars) and *data validation*. Both dBASE and Clipper provide the memvars, but only Clipper provides a built-in validation function.

The proper sequence of events that guarantees safe data entry into any database are as follows:

1. Initialize the memvars
2. Enter data into the memvars
3. Validate the memvar data
4. Open the database file to append the memvar data

The key to these steps being safe is that the database file is only opened for data entry after the memvar data has been checked, and then it is opened for only long enough to add the memvar data.

Memvars must be initialized according to the type of data that they will contain. Memvars that will contain alphanumeric data must be initialized as characters, memvars that will hold numbers as numeric, memvars to hold dates as dates, and so on.

The Sales Management Information System program for order entry (e__ordr.prg) illustrates safe data entry techniques. Memvars are initialized by type, data is entered into the memvars and validated, and then the data is appended to the database file ORDR. The first segment of this program is shown below.

```
* Program . . . . . . . . . . e__ordr
* Description . . . . . . Order Entry
SET COLOR TO W+
    @ 5,0 CLEAR
    @ 3,25 SAY SPACE(30)
    @ 3,35 SAY "ORDER ENTRY"
SET COLOR TO W
```

Remember that the SMIS application contains a multilevel password security system. In the order-entry example, levels 1 and 2 have been selected as being acceptable for customer data entry. Therefore, if the user password has a 1 or 2 access-level assignment, data entry is permitted. If not, then the user is notified by a utility program (u__deny.prg) that access is denied, and the program returns to the orders menu. The $ function searches the character memvar mLEVEL for the proper access level:

```
IF ! "&mAL" $ "12"
    DO u__deny
    RETURN
ENDIF
```

SCREEN APPEARANCE

The field prompts for order entry are displayed on the screen so that the user sees the information that will be required during entry (see Fig. 4-1). All prompts are left-justified, as well as centered on the screen. The centering, as shown in the code below, is determined by the length of the field title plus the longest actual field length (20 for the title plus 20 for the longest field, mCUSTNAME).

```
@ 7,20 SAY "Order Number . . . . . ."
@ 8,20 SAY "Customer Code . . . . ."
@ 9,20 SAY "Customer Name . . . . ."
@10,20 SAY "Salesperson Code . ."
@11,20 SAY "Order Date . . . . . . ."
@12,20 SAY "Quantity . . . . . . . . ."
@13,20 SAY "Item Number . . . . . ."
@14,20 SAY "Description . . . . . ."
```

24

```
┌─────────────────────────────────────────────────────┐
│                                                     │
│   ┌─────────────────────────────────────────────┐   │
│   │     Sales Management Information System      │   │
│   │                 ORDER ENTRY                  │   │
│   └─────────────────────────────────────────────┘   │
│                                                     │
│                                                     │
│        Order Number ......    1                     │
│        Customer Code .....                          │
│        Customer Name .....                          │
│        Salesperson Code ..                          │
│        Order Date ........                          │
│        Quantity ..........                          │
│        Item Number .......                          │
│        Description .......                          │
│        Unit Cost .........                          │
│        Total Cost ........                          │
│                                                     │
│                                                     │
│                                                     │
│              Press [F1] for Help.                   │
│                                                     │
│         Leave blank to return to menu.              │
│                                                     │
└─────────────────────────────────────────────────────┘
```

Fig. 4-1. The order entry initial screen.

```
@15,20 SAY "Unit Cost . . . . . . . . ."
@16,20 SAY "Total Cost . . . . . . . ."
```

MEMVAR INITIALIZATION

The order memvars must be created for data entry. Note, in the code segment below, that each of these memvars is initialized by type. Also note that not all of the displayed information has a memvar, because several of the fields will be derived.

```
STORE SPACE(3)      TO mORDRNR, mCUSTCODE;
                       mSALECODE, mITEMNR
STORE DATE()        TO mDATE
STORE 0             TO mQTY
```

The order number (mORDRNR) is assigned by finding the number of the last order in the ORDR database and then adding one to that number (see the code shown below). If the user is entering the first order, then the order number is automatically assigned a value of one. The function RECCOUNT( ) is used to count the number of records in the database file.

```
USE ORDR INDEX ORDR1
IF RECCOUNT() = 0
    STORE "  1" TO mORDRNR
ELSE
```

```
        STORE STR(VAL(ORDRNR) + 1,3) to mORDRNR
    ENDIF
    USE
```

The order number memvar (mORDRNR) that is generated is then displayed to the user in reverse video:

```
    SET COLOR TO /W
        @ 7,40 SAY mORDRNR
    SET COLOR TO W
```

DATA ENTRY AND VALIDATION

There are two primary ways to accomplish the data-entry task. One is to list all of the user prompts and associated GETS and then use a single READ statement to input the data. Data validation becomes somewhat difficult using this method, however, because the user is allowed to move from one GET to another at will. This freedom of movement is known as full-screen operation. Validation is actually possible, including the ability to use lookup files, by means of Clipper's VALID function and user defined functions. This UDF technique is discussed in Chapter 9.

The second technique of data entry is to follow each GET with an associated READ statement, thus limiting the user to one entry at a time. In this manner, data validation can be performed immediately following each user entry. Additionally, as in the case of the SMIS example, the current user prompt may be highlighted (bright) for enhanced screen appearance.

The user must be allowed to escape from data entry in the event that it is not the activity he or she wishes to perform. Therefore, a provision is made, using the following sequence of commands, to allow the user to enter a blank for the customer code in order to return to the orders menu. The Clipper EMPTY function tests the user entry for a blank. This escape provision is also indicated on the screen during customer code entry; it follows a message that help is available.

```
    Entering = .T.
    DO WHILE Entering
        DO WHILE .T.
            SET COLOR TO W+
                @ 8,20 SAY "Customer Code . . . . ."
            SET COLOR TO W
                @22,31 SAY "Press [F1] for Help."
                @24,26 SAY "Leave blank to return to menu."
                @ 8,40 GET mCUSTCODE PICTURE "@!"
            READ
                @22,0 CLEAR
                @ 8,20 SAY "Customer Code . . . . ."
            IF EMPTY(mCUSTCODE)
                RELEASE ALL
```

```
              @ 5,0 CLEAR
              RETURN
          ENDIF
```

The entered customer code is checked by looking up the code in the customer file CUST. If the entered code is found, the entry is accepted and the customer name is displayed. If the entered code is not found, an error message is displayed by a utility program (u_nofi.prg), and the user is allowed to reenter the customer code:

```
    USE CUST INDEX CUST1
    SEEK mCUSTCODE
    IF ! FOUND( )
        USE
        DO u_nofi
        STORE SPACE(3) TO mCUSTCODE
        LOOP
    ELSE
        SET COLOR TO /W
            @ 9,40 SAY CUSTNAME
        SET COLOR TO W
        USE
        EXIT
    ENDIF
    ENDDO
```

Entry of the salesperson code (mSALECODE) is performed in much the same manner as the customer code entry (see the following code segment). The user is allowed to enter a blank for the salesperson code. If the user enters a code, it is validated by checking the salesperson file SALE.

```
    DO WHILE .T.
        SET COLOR TO W +
            @10,20 SAY "Salesperson Code . ."
        SET COLOR TO W
            @22,31 SAY "Press [F1] for Help"
            @10,40 GET mSALECODE PICTURE "@!"
        READ
        @22,0 CLEAR
        @10,20 SAY "Salesperson Code . ."
        IF EMPTY(mSALECODE)
            EXIT
        ENDIF
        USE SALE INDEX SALE1
        SEEK mSALECODE
        IF ! FOUND( )
            USE
            DO u_nofi
```

```
        STORE SPACE(3) TO mSALECODE
        LOOP
    ELSE
        USE
        EXIT
    ENDIF
ENDDO
```

The order date (mDATE) memvar has already been initialized as the current date, which is displayed in the entry field, as shown below. The date may be changed to any valid date, as long as a date is indeed entered. The Clipper VALID and EMPTY functions are used to ensure that the order date is not left blank.

```
SET COLOR TO W+
    @11,20 SAY "Order Date . . . . . . . ."
SET COLOR TO W
    @11,40 GET mDATE PICTURE "99/99/99";
        VALID ! EMPTY(mDATE)
READ
    @11,20 SAY "Order Date . . . . . . . ."
```

Similarly, the entered quantity (mQTY) is tested to ensure that a zero quantity is not entered:

```
SET COLOR TO W+
    @12,20 SAY "Quantity . . . . . . . . ."
SET COLOR TO W
    @12,40 GET mQTY PICTURE "####";
        VALID ! EMPTY(mQTY)
READ
    @12,20 SAY "Quantity . . . . . . . . ."
```

Several actions occur during entry of the item number (mITEMNR). First, the entered number is checked against the inventory database INVE. If the number is not found, an error message is displayed (u_nofi.prg) and the user is required to reenter an item number. A blank may not be entered, and Help is available.

Because the user may enter "1 ", " 1 ", or " 1" for item number "1", the entered number is converted to " 1" by displaying the character equivalent of the value. This allows the user to enter item numbers more easily.

If the entered number is found, the item description (DESC), unit cost (COST), and total cost are displayed. The total cost is derived by multiplying the unit cost by the quantity (mQTY). Both the unit cost and the total cost are displayed as characters by means of the TRANSFORM function, which also supplies commas to the displayed values. These functions are accomplished by the following sequence of commands.

```
DO WHILE .T.
    SET COLOR TO W+
        @13,20 SAY "Item Number . . . . . . ."
    SET COLOR TO W
        @22,31 SAY "Press [F1] for Help"
        @13,40 GET mITEMNR PICTURE "###";
            VALID ! EMPTY(mITEMNR)
    READ
        @22,0 CLEAR
        @13,20 SAY "Item Number . . . . . . ."
    STORE STR(VAL(mITEMNR),3) TO mITEMNR
    SET COLOR TO /W
        @13,40 SAY mITEMNR
    SET COLOR TO W
    USE INVE INDEX INVE1
    SEEK mITEMNR
    IF ! FOUND( )
        USE
        DO u__nofi
        STORE SPACE(3) TO mITEMNR
        LOOP
    ELSE
        SET COLOR TO /W
            @14,40 SAY DESC
            @15,40 SAY TRANSFORM(COST,"###,###.##")
            @16,40 SAY TRANSFORM(COST*mQTY,"###,###.##")
        SET COLOR TO W
        USE
        EXIT
    ENDIF
ENDDO
Entering = .F.
```

APPENDING DATA

Another utility program (u__entr.prg) consists of a menu that allows the user to add to, change, or ignore the entered data. The command that calls this program is DO u__entr. The choice parameter for this menu is mCHOICE, which was declared PUBLIC in the initialization program (see Fig. 4-2).

The user selection is tested with the CASE function. If the user selects append (mCHOICE = 1), the data is appended to the orders file (ORDR.DBF) before the user is returned to the previous menu. If the user selects change (mCHOICE = 2), the program loops back to the beginning of data entry. If the user selects delete (mCHOICE = 3), the entered data is ignored and the user is returned to the previous menu. The code to handle these choices follows.

The append feature requires additional explanation. If data is deleted from the orders database (using c__ordr.prg), the record is

```
┌─────────────────────────────────────────────────────┐
│  ┌───────────────────────────────────────────────┐  │
│  │   Sales Management Information System          │  │
│  │              ORDER ENTRY                        │  │
│  └───────────────────────────────────────────────┘  │
│                                                      │
│         Order Number ......    1                     │
│         Customer Code .....    AFB                   │
│         Customer Name .....    The AFB Toy Shop      │
│         Salesperson Code ..    JLB                   │
│         Order Date ........    01/02/87              │
│         Quantity ..........    2                     │
│         Item Number .......    1                     │
│         Description .......    Stuffed Bear          │
│         Unit Cost .........       12.50              │
│         Total Cost ........       25.00              │
│                                                      │
│                                                      │
│  ┌───────────────────────────────────────────────┐  │
│  │   Append        Change          Ignore         │  │
│  ├───────────────────────────────────────────────┤  │
│  │   Append (add) this entry to the file          │  │
│  └───────────────────────────────────────────────┘  │
│                                                      │
└─────────────────────────────────────────────────────┘
```

marked with "???" in the order number (ORDRNR) field. Therefore, instead of marking a record for deletion and then PACKing the database file, the record is simply marked for deletion but allowed to remain in the database. Because the variable DELETED is set ON during the initialization program, "???" will never appear in any listing activity. The idea is to SEEK out any "???" records that might exist in the database and then replace the fields of those records with the newly entered data. If no "???" records exist, then a blank record is appended to the database.

There are two reasons for avoiding PACK. First, it takes time to PACK records in a large database, especially when index files exist that must be REINDEXed. Second, it can be risky, because PACKing and REINDEXing have been known to result in corrupted files.

Fig. 4-2. The order-entry completed screen.

```
DO CASE
    CASE mCHOICE = 1
        USE ORDR INDEX ORDR1
        SET DELETED OFF
        SEEK "???"
        IF FOUND( )
            RECALL
        ELSE
            APPEND BLANK
        ENDIF
        REPLACE ORDRNR WITH mORDRNR, CUSTCODE WITH;
            mCUSTCODE, SALECODE WITH mSALECODE,;
            DATE WITH mDATE, QTY WITH mQTY
```

```
                REPLACE ITEMNR WITH mITEMNR
                SET DELETED ON
                USE
                EXIT
            CASE mCHOICE = 2
                Entering = .T.
                LOOP
            CASE mCHOICE = 3
                EXIT
        ENDCASE
    ENDDO Entering
    RELEASE ALL
    @ 5,0 CLEAR
    RETURN
    * End of e__ordr
```

UTILITY ROUTINES

The utility program u__nofi.prg is used to display a "Not Found in files!" message whenever a user entry is not located in a lookup file. The computer bell is sounded, and the error message is displayed (flashing) for three seconds, or until the user presses any key:

```
    * Program . . . . . . . . . u__nofi.prg
    * Description . . . . . . . Not Found Utility
    ? CHR(7)
    SET COLOR TO W + *
        @23,31 SAY 'Not Found in files!'
    SET COLOR TO W
    ? INKEY(3)
    @20,0 CLEAR
    RETURN
    * End of u__nofi.prg
```

The utility program u__infi.prg is used to display an "Already in file!" message whenever the user tries to enter data that already exists in the file:

```
    * Program . . . . . . . . . u__infi.prg
    * Description . . . . . . . Already in File Utility
    ? CHR(7)
    SET COLOR TO W + *
        @23,32 SAY 'Already in file!'
    SET COLOR TO W
    ? INKEY(3)
    @23,0 CLEAR
    RETURN
    * End of u__infi.prg
```

The utility program u_deny.prg is used to display an "Access is Denied!" message whenever the user password has an access level that does not allow a selected activity:

```
* Program . . . . . . . . . u_deny.prg
* Description . . . . . . . Access Denied Utility
CHR(7)
SET COLOR TO W+*
    @23,32 SAY "Access is Denied!"
SET COLOR TO W
? INKEY(3)
@23,0 CLEAR
RETURN
* End of u_deny.prg
```

The utility program u_entr.prg, shown below, is used during data entry to display options to the user after all data has been entered. The program is structured much like the menu programs in Chapter 3, except that the options are displayed horizontally. The right-arrow and left-arrow keys are used to scroll through the choices, and a selection is made by pressing the Enter key or the first key in the name of a choice.

The user may select append (mCHOICE = 1) to add the entered data to a database, change (mCHOICE = 2) to make changes to entered data, or ignore (mCHOICE = 3) to ignore the entry altogether. The menu is contained in a separate window that is displayed at the bottom of the screen. An explanatory message is displayed for each choice.

```
* Program . . . . . . . . . u_entr.prg
* Description . . . . . . . Entry Utility Menu
SET COLOR TO W
    @20,0 CLEAR
    @20,18,24,63 BOX mFRAME1
    @22,18 SAY CHR(195)
    @22,19 SAY REPLICATE(CHR(196),44)
    @22,63 SAY CHR(180)
mCHOICE = 1
SET MESSAGE TO 23
@21,23 PROMPT "Append" MESSAGE SPACE(18)+CHR(179)+;
"  Append (add) this entry to the file.  "+CHR(179)
@21,38 PROMPT "Change" MESSAGE SPACE(18)+CHR(179)+;
"  Make changes to this entry.  "+CHR(179)
@21,53 PROMPT "Ignore" MESSAGE SPACE(18)+CHR(179)+;
"  Ignore this entry & return to menu.  "+CHR(179)
MENU TO mCHOICE
@20,0 CLEAR
RETURN
* End of u_entr.prg
```

Chapter 5

Data-Change Programs

Data-change programs are as critical to database integrity as data entry programs. The rules that apply to data entry equally apply to data change. This chapter discusses the techniques used to safely change and delete database information.

SEQUENCE

The proper sequence of events that guarantees safe data change in a file are basically the same as those discussed for data entry:

1. Open the database file and find the record requiring change.
2. Store the file data in memvars and close the file.
3. Change the memvar data as required.
4. Validate the memvar data.
5. Open the database file, find the record, and replace the data.

The database file is only opened long enough, initially, to transfer the data into memvars. After change and validation, the file is only opened long enough to replace the file data with the memvar data.

The order-change program of the SMIS example is used to demonstrate data-change and data-delete techniques.

```
* Program . . . . . . . . . . c__ordr
* Description . . . . . . . . Order Change/Delete
SET COLOR TO W+
    @ 5,0 CLEAR
    @ 3,25 SAY SPACE(30)
    @ 3,31 SAY "ORDER CHANGE/DELETE"
SET COLOR TO W
```

The SMIS application tests the user password and access level to make sure that order change is allowed. Levels 1 and 2 have been selected as being acceptable for order change. A password access level other than 1 or 2 results in the displaying of an access-denied message (u__deny.prg) followed by a return to the orders menu:

```
IF ! "&mAL" $ "12"
    DO u__deny
    RETURN
ENDIF
```

SCREEN APPEARANCE

The order prompts are displayed on the screen using the following code, arranged identically to those displayed during order entry.

```
@ 7,20 SAY "Order Number . . . . . ."
@ 8,20 SAY "Customer Code . . . . ."
@ 9,20 SAY "Customer Name . . . . ."
@10,20 SAY "Salesperson Code . ."
@11,20 SAY "Order Date . . . . . . . ."
@12,20 SAY "Quantity . . . . . . . . . ."
@13,20 SAY "Item Number . . . . . . ."
@14,20 SAY "Description . . . . . . ."
@15,20 SAY "Unit Cost . . . . . . . ."
@16,20 SAY "Total Cost . . . . . . . ."
```

A memvar is created for the order number (mORDRNR). The user is then prompted to enter the order number that requires change (see the following code segment). Help is available, and the user may enter a blank to return to the orders menu (see Fig. 5-1).

```
STORE SPACE(3) TO mORDRNR
DO WHILE .T.
    SET COLOR TO W+
        @ 7,20 SAY "ORDER Number . . . . . ."
    SET COLOR TO W
        @22,31 SAY "Press [F1] for Help."
        @24,26 SAY "Leave blank to return to menu."
        @ 7,40 GET mORDRNR PICTURE "###"
    READ
```

34

```
+--------------------------------------------------------+
|                                                        |
|     +------------------------------------------+       |
|     |  Sales Management Information System      |       |
|     |          ORDER CHANGE/DELETE              |       |
|     +------------------------------------------+       |
|                                                        |
|                                                        |
|        Order Number ......                             |
|        Customer Code .....                             |
|        Customer Name .....                             |
|        Salesperson Code ..                             |
|        Order Date ........                             |
|        Quantity ..........                             |
|        Item Number .......                             |
|        Description .......                             |
|        Unit Cost .........                             |
|        Total Cost ........                             |
|                                                        |
|                                                        |
|                                                        |
|            Press [F1] for Help.                        |
|                                                        |
|        Leave blank to return to menu.                  |
|                                                        |
+--------------------------------------------------------+
```

Fig. 5-1. The order change/delete screen.

```
IF EMPTY(mORDRNR)
    RELEASE ALL
    @ 5,0 CLEAR
    RETURN
ENDIF
```

Order numbers are actually stored as characters in the database file ORDR. Therefore, the entered order number (mORDRNR) might not be in the proper form. For example, the user might have entered "1 ", " 1 ", or " 1" for the order number. It is necessary to convert the entered number to " 1". This is accomplished by converting the value of the entered number to a character string, and then displaying the result:

```
STORE STR(VAL(mORDRNR),4) TO mORDRNR
SET COLOR TO /W
    @ 7,40 SAY mORDRNR
SET COLOR TO W
```

The database file ORDR is tested to see if the order number exists, using the following sequence of commands. If not, an error message is displayed (u_nofi.prg), the entered order number is replaced with a blank, and the user is returned to order-number entry.

```
USE ORDR INDEX ORDR1
```

```
        SEEK mORDRNR
        IF ! FOUND( )
            USE
            DO u__nofi
            STORE SPACE(3) TO mORDRNR
            LOOP
        ELSE
            EXIT
        ENDIF
    ENDDO
```

MEMVAR INITIALIZATION

Once the entered order number has been found in the ORDR file, the data is stored in data memvars, as shown in the code below. Note that it was not necessary to initialize these memvars earlier in the change program.

```
STORE CUSTCODE      TO mCUSTCODE
STORE SALECODE      TO mSALECODE
STORE QTY           TO mQTY
STORE ITEMNR        TO mITEMNR
STORE DATE          TO mDATE
```

The database file is then closed, and the memvar data is displayed to the user, using the following commands. The numeric memvar (mQTY) must be converted to a character, with the STR function, in order to display only the four-digit quantity.

```
USE
SET COLOR TO /W
        @ 8,40 SAY mCUSTCODE
        @10,40 SAY mSALECODE
        @11,40 SAY mDATE
        @12,40 SAY mITEMNR
        @15,40 SAY STR(mQTY,4)
SET COLOR TO W
```

The customer name must be looked up in the database file CUST and then displayed:

```
USE CUST INDEX CUST1
SEEK mCUSTCODE
IF FOUND( )
        SET COLOR TO /W
            @ 9,40 SAY CUSTNAME
        SET COLOR TO W
ENDIF
USE
```

36

Similarly, the item description and unit cost must be looked up in the database file INVE and then displayed. The total cost is the product of unit cost and quantity. Note that the TRANSFORM function shown in the following code is used to display the unit cost and the total cost.

```
USE INVE INDEX INVE1
SEEK mITEMNR
IF FOUND( )
    SET COLOR TO /W
        @14,40 SAY DESC
        @15,40 SAY TRANSFORM(COST,"###,###.##")
        @16,40 SAY TRANSFORM(COST*mQTY,"###,###.##")
    SET COLOR TO W
ENDIF
USE
```

The utility program (u_chng.prg), called by the command DO u_chng, consists of a menu that allows the user to return to the previous menu without changing or deleting, to change the displayed orders data, or to delete the order (see Fig. 5-2). The choice parameter, mCHOICE, was declared PUBLIC in the initialization program.

The user selection is tested with the CASE function. If the return option is selected (mCHOICE = 1), the user is returned to the orders menu with no changes made. If the change process is selected

Fig. 5-2. The order change/delete options screen.

```
┌─────────────────────────────────────────────────────────┐
│   ┌───────────────────────────────────────────────┐     │
│   │   Sales Management Information System          │     │
│   │          ORDER CHANGE/DELETE                   │     │
│   └───────────────────────────────────────────────┘     │
│                                                          │
│                                                          │
│       Order Number ......    1                           │
│       Customer Code .....    AFB                         │
│       Customer Name .....    The AFB Toy Shop            │
│       Salesperson Code ..    JLB                         │
│       Order Date ........    01/02/87                    │
│       Quantity ..........    2                           │
│       Item Number .......    1                           │
│       Description .......    Stuffed Bear                │
│       Unit Cost .........    12.50                       │
│       Total Cost ........    25.00                       │
│                                                          │
│                                                          │
│   ┌───────────────────────────────────────────────┐     │
│   │   Return         Change         Delete         │     │
│   ├───────────────────────────────────────────────┤     │
│   │   Make no changes and return to menu           │     │
│   └───────────────────────────────────────────────┘     │
└─────────────────────────────────────────────────────────┘
```

(mCHOICE = 2), the user is allowed to change any item except order number. If the user selected delete, the order is deleted from the ORDR file.

The return (mCHOICE = 1) and delete (mCHOICE = 3) selections are tested first, because both result in a return to the previous menu.

```
DO CASE
    CASE mCHOICE = 1
        RELEASE ALL
        @ 5,0 CLEAR
        RETURN
```

DELETION OF DATA

If the user has selected delete, the order number is replaced with "???" and the record is marked for deletion. The database, however, is not PACKed. During the next order number entry, the database will be searched for "???" order numbers. If a record with "???" exists, that record will become the newly entered order:

```
    CASE mCHOICE = 3
        DO u_sure
        IF mSURE $ "Yy"
            USE ORDR INDEX ORDR1
            SEEK mORDRNR
            REPLACE ORDRNR WITH "???"
            DELETE
            USE
        ENDIF
        RELEASE ALL
        @ 5,0 CLEAR
        RETURN
ENDCASE
```

CHANGE AND VALIDATION OF DATA

The remaining selection is change (mCHOICE = 2). It is handled by the sequence of commands shown below. All of the data may be changed with the exception of the order number and the derived fields; however, the derived fields are recalculated and displayed if changes are made. Data change proceeds much like data entry, except that a blank may not be entered for the customer code.

```
Changing = .T.
DO WHILE Changing
    DO WHILE .T.
        SET COLOR TO W+
            @ 8,20 SAY "Customer Code . . . . ."
        SET COLOR TO W
```

```
            @22,30 SAY "Press [F1] for Help."
            @ 8,40 GET mCUSTCODE PICTURE "@!";
                    VALID ! EMPTY(mCUSTCODE)
    READ
            @22,0 CLEAR
            @ 8,20 SAY "Customer Code . . . . ."
```

Note that the Clipper VALID function is used to test for a blank customer code (mCUSTCODE). If the user enters a blank for the customer code, the entry will not be accepted by the VALID function. Otherwise, the entered code is checked in the customer file, as shown below.

```
        USE CUST INDEX CUST1
        SEEK mCUSTCODE
        IF ! FOUND( )
            USE
            DO u_nofi
            STORE SPACE(3) TO mCUSTCODE
            LOOP
        ELSE
            SET COLOR TO /W
                @ 9,40 SAY CUSTNAME
            SET COLOR TO W
            USE
            EXIT
        ENDIF
    ENDDO
```

Similarly, a loop is set up for the salesperson code (mSALECODE). A blank entry, however, is allowed for the salesperson code:

```
    DO WHILE .T.
        SET COLOR TO W+
            @10,20 SAY "Salesperson Code . ."
        SET COLOR TO W
            @22,30 SAY "Press [F1] for Help"
            @10,40 GET mSALECODE PICTURE "@!"
        READ
            @22,0 CLEAR
            @10,20 SAY "Salesperson Code . ."
        IF EMPTY(mSALECODE)
            EXIT
        ENDIF
        USE SALE INDEX SALE1
        SEEK mSALECODE
        IF ! FOUND( )
            USE
            DO u_nofi
```

```
                STORE SPACE(3) TO mSALECODE
                LOOP
            ELSE
                USE
                EXIT
            ENDIF
        ENDDO
```

A blank date is not allowed, and is tested by the Clipper VALID and EMPTY functions:

```
        SET COLOR TO W+
            @11,20 SAY "Order Date . . . . . . . ."
        SET COLOR TO W
            @11,40 GET mDATE PICTURE "99/99/99";
                VALID ! EMPTY(mDATE)
        READ
            @11,20 SAY "Order Date . . . . . . . ."
```

A zero quantity (mQTY) is not allowed, and is also tested by the VALID and EMPTY functions:

```
        SET COLOR TO W+
            @12,20 SAY "Quantity . . . . . . . . ."
        SET COLOR TO W
            @12,40 GET mQTY PICTURE "####";
                VALID ! EMPTY(mQTY)
        READ
            @12,20 SAY "Quantity . . . . . . . . ."
```

The item number (mITEMNR) is tested by looking up the entered number in the inventory file. If the item number is found in the file, the description and unit cost are displayed, along with the derived total cost. This is accomplished with the following code.

```
        DO WHILE .T.
            SET COLOR TO W+
                @13,20 SAY "Item Number . . . . . . ."
            SET COLOR TO W
                @22,30 SAY "Press [F1] for Help"
                @13,40 GET mITEMNR PICTURE "###";
                    VALID ! EMPTY(mITEMNR)
            READ
                @22,0 CLEAR
                @13,20 SAY "Item Number . . . . . . ."
            STORE STR(VAL(mITEMNR),3) TO mITEMNR
            SET COLOR TO /W
                @13,40 SAY mITEMNR
            SET COLOR TO W
            USE INVE INDEX INVE1
```

```
SEEK mITEMNR
IF ! FOUND()
    USE
    DO u__nofi
    STORE SPACE(3) TO mITEMNR
    LOOP
ELSE
    SET COLOR TO /W
        @14,40 SAY DESC
        @15,40 SAY TRANSFORM(COST,"###,###.##")
        @16,40 SAY TRANSFORM(COST*mQTY,"###,###.##")
    SET COLOR TO W
    USE
    EXIT
    ENDIF
ENDDO
Changing = .F.
```

UPDATING DATA

Within the changing loop, a different menu is displayed. The utility program (u__upda.prg) allows the user to update, change, or ignore the displayed order data (see Fig. 5-3).

The user selection is tested with the CASE function, as shown below. If the user selects update (mCHOICE = 1), the order number is found in the ORDR database and the data is changed as displayed.

Fig. 5-3. The order update screen.

```
┌──────────────────────────────────────────────────────────────┐
│                                                                │
│     ┌────────────────────────────────────────────────┐        │
│     │    Sales Management Information System           │       │
│     │           ORDER CHANGE/DELETE                    │       │
│     └────────────────────────────────────────────────┘        │
│                                                                │
│        Order Number ......   1                                 │
│        Customer Code .....  AFB                                │
│        Customer Name .....  The AFB Toy Shop                   │
│        Salesperson Code ..  JLB                                │
│        Order Date ........  01/02/87                           │
│        Quantity ..........   2                                 │
│        Item Number .......   1                                 │
│        Description .......  Stuffed Bear                       │
│        Unit Cost .........     12.50                           │
│        Total Cost ........     25.00                           │
│                                                                │
│                                                                │
│     ┌────────────────────────────────────────────────┐        │
│     │  Update         Change         Ignore           │       │
│     ├────────────────────────────────────────────────┤       │
│     │      Update file with changes made              │       │
│     └────────────────────────────────────────────────┘        │
│                                                                │
└──────────────────────────────────────────────────────────────┘
```

If the user selects change (mCHOICE = 2), the user is allowed to continue making changes. If the user selects ignore, the changes made are ignored.

```
DO u_upda
DO CASE
    CASE mCHOICE = 1
        USE ORDR INDEX ORDR1
        SEEK mORDRNR
        REPLACE CUSTCODE WITH mCUSTCODE, SALECODE;
            WITH mSALECODE, DATE WITH mDATE, QTY WITH;
            mQTY, ITEMNR WITH mITEMNR
        USE
        EXIT
    CASE mCHOICE = 2
        Changing = .T.
        LOOP
    CASE mCHOICE = 3
        EXIT
    ENDCASE
ENDDO Changing
RELEASE ALL
@ 5,0 CLEAR
RETURN
* End of c_ordr
```

UTILITY ROUTINES

The utility program u_chng.prg is used during data change to display options to the user after the original data has been located in the file. The program is structured much like the menu programs in Chapter 3, except that the options are displayed horizontally. The right-arrow and left-arrow keys are used to scroll through the choices, and a selection is made by pressing the Enter key or the first key in the name of a choice.

The user may select return (mCHOICE = 1) to return to the previous menu with making any changes in the data, change (mCHOICE = 2) to make changes, or delete (mCHOICE = 3) to delete the information from the database:

```
* Program . . . . . . . . . . u_chng.prg
* Description . . . . . . Change Utility Menu
SET COLOR TO W
    @20,0 CLEAR
    @20,18,24,63 BOX mFRAME1
    @22,18 SAY CHR(195)
    @22,19 SAY REPLICATE(CHR(196),44)
    @22,63 SAY CHR(180)
```

```
mCHOICE = 1
SET MESSAGE TO 23
@21,23 PROMPT "Return"   MESSAGE SPACE(18)+CHR(179)+;
"  Make no changes and return to menu.   "+CHR(179)
@21,38 PROMPT "Change"   MESSAGE SPACE(18)+CHR(179)+;
"  Make changes to this entry.   "+CHR(179)
@21,53 PROMPT "Delete"   MESSAGE SPACE(18)+CHR(179)+;
"  Delete this entry.   "+CHR(179)
MENU TO mCHOICE
@20,0 CLEAR
RETURN
* End of u_chng.prg
```

The utility program u_upda.prg is used during data change to display options to the user after the data has been changed. Again, the user may select update (mCHOICE = 1) to update the database with the changes made, change (mCHOICE = 2) to continue making changes, or ignore (mCHOICE = 3) to ignore the changes made and return to the previous menu:

```
* Program . . . . . . . . .. . u_upda.prg
* Description . . . . . . Update Utility Menu
SET COLOR TO W
    @20,0 CLEAR
    @20,18,24,63 BOX mFRAME1
    @22,18 SAY CHR(195)
    @22,19 SAY REPLICATE(CHR(196),44)
    @22,63 SAY CHR(180)
mCHOICE = 1
SET MESSAGE TO 23
@21,23 PROMPT "Update" MESSAGE SPACE(18)+CHR(179)+;
"  Update file with changes made.   "+CHR(179)
@21,38 PROMPT "Change" MESSAGE SPACE(18)+CHR(179)+;
"  Make additional changes to this entry. "+CHR(179)
@21,53 PROMPT "Ignore"   MESSAGE SPACE(18)+CHR(179)+;
"  Ignore changes & return to menu.   "+CHR(179)
MENU TO mCHOICE
@20,0 CLEAR
RETURN
* End of u_upda.prg
```

The utility program u_sure.prg, shown below, is used when the choice to delete has been selected. It requires the user to press the Y or N key to confirm or cancel the delete action. The memvar mSURE is returned to the calling program.

```
* Program . . . . . . . . . . u_sure.prg
* Description . . . . . . Are You Sure Utility

? CHR(7)
```

```
SET COLOR TO W
    @23,31 SAY "Are You Sure (Y/N)?"
DO WHILE .T.
    WAIT "" TO mSURE
    IF mSURE $ "YyNn"
        EXIT
    ELSE
        LOOP
    ENDIF
ENDDO
@23,0 CLEAR
RETURN
* End of u__sure.prg
```

Chapter 6

Data List/Print Programs

A very important feature of any applications program is the manner in which database information is displayed. A single database might need to be listed many different ways, according to special user instructions. It might also be necessary to furnish a formal report printout. This chapter discusses several different data-listing circumstances, including listing data according to selected criteria, and report printing.

SCREEN APPEARANCE

Data is usually listed in tabular form. A heading is displayed, and then the data is displayed in columns below the heading. If more than one *page* (display screen) of data exists in the file, the user must be able to move forward and backward in the database at will.

The customer listing program (l_cust.prg) of the Sales Management Information System is an example of a basic data-listing procedure.

```
* Program . . . . . . . . . . l_cust.prg
* Description . . . . . . . . . Customer List
SET COLOR TO W+
     @ 5,0  CLEAR
     @ 3,25 SAY SPACE(30)
```

```
      @ 3,33 SAY "LIST CUSTOMERS"
SET COLOR TO W
```

The password access levels that are acceptable for customer listing are 1, 2, and 3. If the user password has an unacceptable access level, the user is notified by a utility program (u__deny.prg) as follows.

```
IF ! "&mAL" $ "123"
    DO u__deny
    RETURN
ENDIF
```

The customer information displayed includes the customer code, customer name, and phone number. The column headings are displayed in highlighted (bright) video:

```
SET COLOR TO W+
    @ 6,21 SAY "Code  Customer Name     Phone  "
    @ 7,21 SAY "==== ==================== ============"
SET COLOR TO W
```

The PUBLIC memvar mCHOICE is initialized for use later, in the utility program that displays the user choices.

```
mCHOICE = 6
```

LISTING DATA

The customer information exists in the database file CUST, which is indexed on customer code (CUSTCODE) to the file CUST1, using the following command. Therefore, the customer data will be displayed in order of customer code.

```
USE CUST INDEX CUST1
```

The data display activity is enclosed in a DO WHILE loop, shown below, so that the user can EXIT when desired. Customer data is displayed in groups of ten customers, each group making up a screen, or page, of data. The display starts on line 9.

```
DO WHILE ! EOF( )
    @ 8,0
    DISPLAY OFF NEXT 10 SPACE(20)+CUSTCODE+" ",CUSTNAME,;
        PHONE
```

After a page of data, consisting of ten or fewer customers, is

```
┌─────────────────────────────────────────────────────┐
│   ┌───────────────────────────────────────────────┐ │
│   │   Sales Management Information System          │ │
│   │            LIST CUSTOMERS                      │ │
│   └───────────────────────────────────────────────┘ │
│                                                       │
│                                                       │
│   Code      Customer Name        Phone               │
│   ====  ==================== ============            │
│                                                       │
│   AFB   The AFB Toy Shop      123-555-8899           │
│   JAB   JAB Disney Supplies   123-555-1121           │
│                                                       │
│                                                       │
│   ┌───────────────────────────────────────────────┐ │
│   │ Forward   Backward   Top   End   Print  Return │ │
│   ├───────────────────────────────────────────────┤ │
│   │       Return to the previous menu              │ │
│   └───────────────────────────────────────────────┘ │
└─────────────────────────────────────────────────────┘
```

Fig. 6-1. The list customers screen.

displayed, another utility program (u__list.prg) is called to display the user choices. There are six different choices that are displayed in menu format. These are forward, backward, top, end, print, and return (see Fig. 6-1).

The memvar mCHOICE was initialized earlier to a value equal to the return selection (mCHOICE = 6). If there is no data in the customer file, the user will be automatically returned to the customer menu.

If the end of the file is reached, the menu automatically highlights the return choice (mCHOICE = 6), thereby indicating to the user that the end of the file is currently displayed. Otherwise, the page-forward choice (mCHOICE = 1) is highlighted:

```
IF EOF( )
    mCHOICE = 6
ELSE
    mCHOICE = 1
ENDIF
DO u__list
```

The DO CASE command is the next command executed. It is used to test the user selection. Again, there are six possible selections to look for.

If the user decides to go forward, the screen is cleared below the column headings and the next ten customers are displayed. If the user selects forward when the end of file has been reached, the beginning of the file is again displayed, using the GO TOP command:

```
CASE mCHOICE = 1   && Page Forward
    @ 8,0 CLEAR
    IF EOF( )
        GO TOP
    ENDIF
    LOOP
```

If the user selects backward, then it is necessary to skip backwards in the customer file. Because ten (or fewer) customers are currently being displayed, going back ten records will just display the current ten customers again. Therefore, the skip backwards procedure is accomplished in three steps: skip backwards, test for beginning-of-file (BOF), and skip backwards again.

Note, in the following code, that 16 total records are skipped, to allow the user to use both forward and backward selections to position a particular group of records on the screen at one time.

```
CASE mCHOICE = 2   && Page Backward
    @ 8,0 CLEAR
    SKIP-8
    IF ! BOF( )
        SKIP-8
    ENDIF
    LOOP
```

If the user selects top (mCHOICE = 3), then the first 10 customers in the indexed file are displayed:

```
CASE mCHOICE = 3   && Go to top of file
    GO TOP
    LOOP
```

If the user selects end (mCHOICE = 4), then the last 10 customers in the indexed file are displayed, using the following sequence of commands. Note that this requires a GO BOTTOM command followed by a skip backwards.

```
CASE mCHOICE = 4   && Go to end of file
    GO BOTTOM
    SKIP-8
    LOOP
```

If the selection is to print (mCHOICE = 5), the displayed information remains and the listing loop is exited:

```
        CASE mCHOICE = 5   && Print the file
            EXIT
```

If the user selects return (mCHOICE = 6), the database is closed, the screen is cleared, and the user is returned to the customer menu:

```
        CASE mCHOICE = 6   && Return to previous menu
            RELEASE ALL
            USE
            @ 5,0 CLEAR
            RETURN
        ENDCASE
    ENDDO
```

The only way to exit the listing loop, other than returning to the previous menu, is by selecting the print choice.

PRINTING DATA

Before attempting to print the list of customers, it is necessary to check to make sure that a printer is connected and online. The EXTENDA utility of Clipper includes a user-defined function (see Chapter 9) called ISPRINTER( ) that does the error check. This is an assembly-language routine that is supplied with Clipper as a separate object-code file. It must be linked with the SMIS object during compilation (see Chapters 10 and 11).

If the printer is not ready, as detected by ISPRINTER( ), an error message is displayed and the user is returned to the customer menu, using the code shown below.

```
IF mCHOICE = 5
    IF ! ISPRINTER( )
        ? CHR(7)
        SET COLOR TO W + *
            @22,30 SAY "Printer Not Ready!"
        SET COLOR TO W
        USE
        ? INKEY(5)
        RELEASE ALL
        @ 5,0 CLEAR
        RETURN
    ENDIF
```

There are two methods that can be used to print a database file. The first uses the Clipper REPORT FORM generator, which creates a file that contains the printout specifications. This method has its disadvantages.

For one thing, the format files are separate from the executable program, and therefore must be distributed with each copy of the application. The SMIS example would then require that six different programs exist on the distribution diskette. These would be the main file (SMIS.EXE), and five printout format files: cust.frm, ordr.frm, inve.frm, sale.frm, and pass.frm.

A second disadvantage is that the REPORT FORM generator does not always provide enough flexibility in report formatting, particularly when it comes to special report headings that might require use of a memvar name.

The second method consists of incorporating the report printing instructions in the program itself. This way, the distribution diskette does not require any program files other than the main executable program. All of the report routines in the SMIS example include this printout code.

If the printer is ready, the printing operation begins. The memvar mLINE represents the number of lines printed, and another memvar, mPAGE, represents the number of pages.

The console is set OFF to prevent the listing from being displayed during printing. The output of the file is directed to the printer with SET PRINT ON, and the record pointer is sent to the top of the file with GO TOP:

```
@20,0  CLEAR
SET COLOR TO W + *
    @22,30 SAY "Printing..."
SET CONSOLE OFF
STORE 50 TO mLINE
STORE 0 TO mPAGE
SET PRINT ON
GO TOP
```

The printing routine is contained in a DO WHILE loop, shown below. A report title and the column headings are required for each page of the printout. If the line number exceeds 40 (mLINE > 40), then the printer is sent a page eject with ? CHR(12), and the header information is printed on a new page. After a page eject, the page number (mPAGE) is incremented by one and the line number (mLINE) is reset to one. Note that the first page of the report also contains the header information, because mLINE was initialized to 50; however, the initial page eject is suppressed.

```
DO WHILE ! EOF( )
    IF mLINE > 40
        IF mPAGE > 0
            ? CHR(12)
        ENDIF
        STORE 1 TO mLINE
        STORE mPAGE + 1 TO mPAGE
```

```
? "   Page No. "+STR(mPAGE,3)
? "   ",DATE( )
?
? SPACE(23)+"Sales Management Information System"
?
?
?
? SPACE(36)+"Customers"
?
?
? SPACE(21)+"Code   Customer Name   "+;
   "    Phone     "
? SPACE(21)+" = = =   = = = = = = = = = = = = = ="+;
   " = = = = = = = = = = = ="
ENDIF
```

The customer code, name, and telephone number are printed, and the line counter (mLINE) is incremented after each customer output:

```
? SPACE(21)+CUSTCODE+" ",CUSTNAME,PHONE
STORE mLINE+1 TO mLINE
SKIP
ENDDO
```

The loop is exited after the entire customer file has been printed. The last page is then ejected, the file is closed, and the user is returned to the customer menu:

```
? CHR(12)
SET PRINT OFF
SET CONSOLE ON
ENDIF
USE
RELEASE ALL
@ 5,0 CLEAR
RETURN
* End of l_cust.prg
```

An example of a finished customers report is shown in Fig. 6-2.

SELECTION CRITERIA

The list/print program for orders (l_ordr.prg) of the Sales Management System example differs from the previous customer program. First, it uses a parameter that is passed from the orders menu (m_ordr.prg). This parameter determines the list/print criteria. Second, it uses two open database files from which to extract the list/print information.

```
Page No.   1
01/02/87

            Sales Management Information System


                        Customers


        Code    Customer Name          Phone
        ====    ====================   ============

        AFB   The AFB Toy Shop       123-555-8899
        JAB   JAB Disney Supplies    123-555-1121
```

Fig. 6-2. The customers print-out.

The parameter that is passed from the orders menu is ordr2. If ordr2 equals 1, all orders are listed. If ordr2 is equal to 2, a valid customer code must first be entered, and then orders for only that customer are listed. If ordr2 equals 3, an item code must be entered to produce an orders listing for that item. Finally, if ordr2 is 4, orders for a selected salesperson are listed. Note that the passed parameter must be identified by the statement PARAMETERS ordr2, as shown in the following code segment.

```
* Program . . . . . . . . . . l_ordr.prg
* Description . . . . . . . . Orders List

PARAMETERS ordr2
SET COLOR TO W+
    @ 5,0   CLEAR
    @ 3,25 SAY SPACE(30)
    @ 3,35 SAY "LIST ORDERS"
SET COLOR TO W
IF ! "&mAL" $ "123"
    DO u_deny
    RETURN
ENDIF
```

The DO CASE command is used to see what the user selected from the orders menu. If the user selected 2 as the value of ordr2, then customer code entry is required. If 3 was selected, item number entry is required, and for 4, the salesperson code must be entered. Note, in the code shown below, that each entry includes an escape provision, with the Clipper EMPTY( ) function, as well as entry validation.

```
DO CASE
    CASE ordr2 = 2
        STORE SPACE(3) TO mCUSTCODE
        DO WHILE .T.
            SET COLOR TO W+
                @ 7,29 SAY "Customer Code . . . . . "
            SET COLOR TO W
                @22,30 SAY "Press [F1] for Help."
                @24,25 SAY "Leave blank to return to menu."
                @ 7,49 GET mCUSTCODE PICTURE "@!"
            READ
                @22,0 CLEAR
                @ 7,29 SAY "Customer Code . . . . . "
            IF EMPTY(mCUSTCODE)
                RELEASE ALL
                @ 5,0 CLEAR
                RETURN
            ENDIF
            USE CUST INDEX CUST1
        SEEK mCUSTCODE
        IF ! FOUND( )
            USE
            DO u__nofi
            STORE SPACE(3) TO mCUSTCODE
            LOOP
        ELSE
            USE
            EXIT
        ENDIF
        ENDDO
    CASE ordr2 = 3
        STORE SPACE(3) TO mITEMNR
        DO WHILE .T.
            SET COLOR TO W+
                @ 7,29 SAY "Item Number . . . . . . . "
            SET COLOR TO W
                @22,30 SAY "Press [F1] for Help."
                @24,25 SAY "Leave blank to return to menu."
                @ 7,49 GET mITEMNR PICTURE "###"
            READ
                @22,0 CLEAR
                @ 7,29 SAY "Item Number . . . . . . . "
            IF EMPTY(mITEMNR)
                RELEASE ALL
```

```
                    @ 5,0 CLEAR
                    RETURN
                    ENDIF
                    USE INVE INDEX INVE1
                    SEEK mITEMNR
                    IF ! FOUND( )
                         USE
                         DO u__nofi
                         STORE SPACE(3) TO mITEMNR
                         LOOP
                    ELSE
                         USE
                         EXIT
                    ENDIF
               ENDDO
          CASE ordr2 = 4
               STORE SPACE(3) TO mSALECODE
               DO WHILE .T.
                    SET COLOR TO W+
                         @ 7,29 SAY "Salesperson Code . . "
                    SET COLOR TO W
                         @22,30 SAY "Press [F1] for Help."
                         @24,25 SAY "Leave blank to return to menu."
                         @ 7,49 GET mSALECODE PICTURE "@!"
                    READ
                         @22,0 CLEAR
                         @ 7,29 SAY "Salesperson Code . . "
                    IF EMPTY(mSALECODE)
                         RELEASE ALL
                         @ 5,0 CLEAR
                         RETURN
                    ENDIF
                    USE SALE INDEX SALE1
                    SEEK mSALECODE
                    IF ! FOUND( )
                         USE
                         DO u__nofi
                         STORE SPACE(3) TO mSALECODE
                         LOOP
                    ELSE
                         USE
                         EXIT
                    ENDIF
               ENDDO
          OTHERWISE
     ENDCASE
```

The column headings are displayed in bright video using the commands shown below. The displayed information includes order number, customer code, salesperson code, order date, item number,

and total cost.

```
SET COLOR TO W+
   @ 6,17 SAY "Order# Cust Sale   Date   Item " +;
              "Quan Total Cost"
   @ 7,17 SAY " = = = = = =  = = = =  = = = =  = = = = = = = =
              = = = = " +; " = = = =  = = = = = = = = = ="
SET COLOR TO W
```

There are two techniques that may be used to display the order file according to a selected criteria. The first uses the SET FILTER TO command. A filter condition is created according to the orders menu parameter ORDR2:

```
SELECT 1
USE ORDR INDEX ORDR1
DO CASE
    CASE ordr2 = 2
        SET FILTER TO CUSTCODE = mCUSTCODE
    CASE ordr2 = 3
        SET FILTER TO ITEMNR = mITEMNR
    CASE ordr2 = 4
        SET FILTER TO SALECODE = mSALECODE
    OTHERWISE
ENDCASE
GO TOP
```

The second technique (which is recommended, especially for larger databases) involves copying the database file ORDR to a temporary database file called TEMP. This file is organized according to the selected criteria. This results in faster execution during listing. This method is shown in the following code segment.

The Clipper COPY TO command allows for the inclusion of a FOR condition. The file structure of the temporary file TEMP is identical to that of ORDR. The indexed version of the orders database also results in a sorted temporary file.

```
USE ORDR INDEX ORDR1
DO CASE
    CASE ordr2 = 2
        COPY TO TEMP FOR CUSTCODE = mCUSTCODE
    CASE ordr2 = 3
        COPY TO TEMP FOR ITEMNR = ITEMNR
    CASE ordr2 = 4
        COPY TO TEMP FOR SALECODE = mSALECODE
    OTHERWISE
ENDCASE
USE
```

All of the displayed information exists in the database file ORDR (or TEMP) with the exception of the total cost. It is necessary to derive the total cost, using the value of the quantity field, in the database file ORDR (or TEMP), multiplied by the unit cost, stored in the database file INVE. These two files can be linked on the item number (ITEMNR) in order to derive the total cost.

Two work areas must be specified, using the following commands, in order to make the proper link. Work area two (alias B) is selected for the inventory lookup file INVE. Work area one contains the orders file.

```
SELECT 2
USE INVE INDEX INVE1
SELECT 1
IF ordr2 = 1
    USE ORDR INDEX ORDR1
ELSE
    USE TEMP
ENDIF
SET RELATION TO ITEMNR INTO B
```

The information is displayed in tabular form (see Fig. 6-3). The derived total cost is calculated by multiplying the quantity times the unit cost from the alias file B. The TRANSFORM function is used to display the total cost:

```
DO WHILE .T.
    @ 8,0
    DISPLAY OFF NEXT 10 SPACE(18)+ORDRNR+" ",;
        CUSTCODE+" ",SALECODE+" ",DATE,ITEMNR+" ",QTY,;
        TRANSFORM(QTY*B->COST,"###,###.##")
    IF EOF( )
        mCHOICE = 6
    ELSE
        mCHOICE = 1
    ENDIF
    DO u_list
    DO CASE
        CASE mCHOICE = 1    && Page Forward
            @ 8,0 CLEAR
            IF EOF( )
                GO TOP
            ENDIF
            LOOP
        CASE mCHOICE = 2    && Page Backward
            @ 8,0 CLEAR
            SKIP-8
```

```
        Sales Management Information System
                   LIST ORDERS
```

```
Ordr # Cust Sale   Date    Item Quan Total Cost
====== ==== ==== ======== ==== ==== ==========
     1  AFB  JLB  01/02/87   1    2      25.00
     2  JAB  JLB  01/02/87   1    1      12.50
```

```
 Forward    Backward    Top    End    Print    Return
           Return to the previous menu
```

Fig. 6-3. The list orders screen.

```
                    IF ! BOF( )
                        SKIP-8
                    ENDIF
                    LOOP
                CASE mCHOICE = 3  && Go to top of file
                    GO TOP
                    LOOP
                CASE mCHOICE = 4  && Go to end of file
                    GO BOTTOM
                    SKIP-8
                    LOOP
                CASE mCHOICE = 5  && Print the file
                    EXIT
                CASE mCHOICE = 6  && Return to previous menu
                    RELEASE ALL
                    USE
                    @ 5,0 CLEAR
                    RETURN
            ENDCASE
        ENDDO
        * End of l_ordr.prg (partial)
```

The print routine uses the same principles as discussed for the customer printout, and is included in the full source code in Appendix A.

UTILITY ROUTINES

The utility program u_list.prg, that follows, is used during the process of listing data to display the options to the user. The user may select forward (mCHOICE = 1) to display the next page (10 records), backward (mCHOICE = 2) to display the previous page, top (mCHOICE = 3) to go to the top of the file, end (mCHOICE = 4) to go to the end of the file, print (mCHOICE = 5) to print the file, or return (mCHOICE = 6) to return to the previous menu. The menu is enclosed in a window that displays explanatory messages as the user scrolls by each choice.

```
* Program . . . . . . . . . . u_list.prg
* Description . . . . . . List Utility Menu
SET COLOR TO W
    @20,0 CLEAR
    @20,17,24,62 BOX mFRAME1
    @22,17 SAY CHR(195)
    @22,18 SAY REPLICATE(CHR(196),44)
    @22,62 SAY CHR(180)
SET MESSAGE TO 23
    @21,19 PROMPT "Forward"   MESSAGE SPACE(17)+CHR(179)+;
"  Page forward in this file.   "+CHR(179)
    @21,28 PROMPT "Backward"   MESSAGE SPACE(17)+CHR(179)+;
"  Page backward in this file.   "+CHR(179)
    @21,38 PROMPT "Top"   MESSAGE SPACE(17)+CHR(179)+;
"  Go to the TOP of this file.   "+CHR(179)
    @21,43 PROMPT "End"   MESSAGE SPACE(17)+CHR(179)+;
"  Go to the END of this file.   "+CHR(179)
    @21,48 PROMPT "Print"   MESSAGE SPACE(17)+CHR(179)+;
"  Print this file.   "+CHR(179)
    @21,55 PROMPT "Return"   MESSAGE  SPACE(17)+CHR(179)+;
"  Return to the previous menu.   "+CHR(179)
MENU TO mCHOICE
@20,0 CLEAR
RETURN
* End of u_list.prg
```

Chapter 7

Data Backup Programs

An applications program is normally designed to track and maintain a significant amount of data. The larger a database becomes, the greater the fear of losing that data. The safe approach to alleviating the fear is to regularly maintain data, using backups. This chapter will describe a simple method of letting the user back up data from a fixed drive to a floppy diskette, as well as recall that data if need be.

MAKING A BACKUP TO A DISKETTE

A backup menu (see Fig. 7-1) for the Sales Management Information example is included as an option from the main menu. The user can select the backup choice, insert the backup diskette into the floppy drive, and then continue with the backup procedure.

The backup program (b_data.prg) has some disadvantages, due to the fact that certain DOS-type commands and functions cannot be included in the Clipper code. For example, the Clipper program itself cannot check for a full diskette, a faulty drive, or an unformatted diskette. Such errors result in a non-Clipper error message from DOS. The discussion on UDFs in Chapter 9 offers some suggestions on how such errors could be handled.

The backup program shown below notifies the user that a diskette must be installed into floppy drive A. The user must then press a key to continue with the backup (see Fig. 7-2).

```
+--------------------------------------------------------+
|                                                        |
|   +------------------------------------------------+   |
|   |  Sales Management Information System           |   |
|   |  DATA BACKUP MENU                              |   |
|   +------------------------------------------------+   |
|                                                        |
|                                                        |
|              Backup                                    |
|              Install                                   |
|              Create                                    |
|                                                        |
|                                                        |
|                                                        |
|                                                        |
|                                                        |
|          Backup Data to Diskette                       |
|                                                        |
+--------------------------------------------------------+
```

Fig. 7-1. The data
backup menu screen.

```
+--------------------------------------------------------+
|                                                        |
|   +------------------------------------------------+   |
|   |  Sales Management Information System           |   |
|   |  DATA BACKUP MENU                              |   |
|   +------------------------------------------------+   |
|                                                        |
|                                                        |
|     Data will be backed up to floppy drive A.          |
|                                                        |
|     Insert SMIS backup diskette in drive A.            |
|                                                        |
|                                                        |
|     Press any key when ready to continue ....          |
|                                                        |
|                                                        |
|                                                        |
|                                                        |
+--------------------------------------------------------+
```

Fig. 7-2. The data
backup screen.

```
* Program . . . . . . . . . . b__data.prg
* Description . . . . . . . . . . Backup to Floppy
SET COLOR TO W+
    @ 5,0 CLEAR
    @ 3,25 SAY SPACE(30)
    @ 3,35 SAY "DATA BACKUP"
SET COLOR TO W
@ 9,20 SAY "Data will be backed up to floppy drive A."
@11,20 SAY " Insert SMIS backup diskette in drive A. "
@14,20 SAY "Press any key when ready to continue . . . ."
? INKEY(0)
    @10,0 CLEAR
SET COLOR TO W+*
    @22,26 SAY 'P l e a s e   W a i t . . .'
SET COLOR TO W
SET CONSOLE OFF
```

The **COPY FILE** command copies each database file to the diskette in drive A. The DOS-type command >NUL suppresses the customary "1 file copied . . ." message that is displayed after each file is copied:

```
COPY FILE ORDR.DBF TO A:ORDR.DBF>NUL
COPY FILE INVE.DBF TO A:INVE.DBF>NUL
COPY FILE SALE.DBF TO A:SALE.DBF>NUL
COPY FILE CUST.DBF TO A:CUST.DBF>NUL
COPY FILE PASSWORD.DBF TO A:PASSWORD.DBF>NUL
SET CONSOLE ON
RELEASE ALL
@ 5,0 CLEAR
RETURN
* End of b__data.prg
```

INSTALLING BACKUP DATA

Backup data can be recalled from floppy diskette and installed on the fixed drive in a similar manner. Again, the user is notified that the backup diskette must be properly placed into the floppy drive A. The user must again press any key to continue (see Fig. 7-3).

The recall/install program (r__data.prg) does make sure that the correct backup diskette has been placed in the floppy drive. The FILE function checks for the existence of the database file ORDR on the diskette. If that file is not found, then the user is notified of the error and is returned to the backup menu. The code used to execute these activities is shown below.

```
* Program . . . . . . . . . . r__data.prg
* Description . . . . . . . . . . Recall Floppy Data
```

```
┌─────────────────────────────────────────────────────────────┐
│                                                             │
│        ┌──────────────────────────────────────────┐         │
│        │  Sales Management Information System       │         │
│        │  DATA RECALL MENU                          │         │
│        └──────────────────────────────────────────┘         │
│                                                             │
│                                                             │
│         Data will be recalled from floppy drive A.          │
│                                                             │
│         Insert SMIS backup diskette in drive A.             │
│                                                             │
│                                                             │
│         Press any key when ready to continue ....           │
│                                                             │
│                                                             │
│                                                             │
│                                                             │
│                                                             │
│                                                             │
│                                                             │
│                                                             │
└─────────────────────────────────────────────────────────────┘
```

Fig. 7-3. The data recall screen.

```
SET COLOR TO W+
    @ 5,0 CLEAR
    @ 3,25 SAY SPACE(30)
    @ 3,35 SAY "DATA RECALL"
SET COLOR TO W
@ 9,19 SAY "Data will be recalled from floppy drive A."
@11,19 SAY " Insert SMIS backup diskette in drive A. "
@14,19 SAY " Press any key when ready to continue . . . ."
? INKEY(0)
    @10,0   CLEAR
IF ! FILE("A:ORDR.DBF")
? CHR(7)
SET COLOR TO W+
        @22,23 SAY "Data not found on floppy diskette."
    SET COLOR TO W
        ? INKEY(5)
        @ 5,0 CLEAR
        RETURN
ENDIF
SET COLOR TO W+*
    @22,26 SAY 'P l e a s e   W a i t . . .'
SET COLOR TO W
```

The actual installation, performed by the following commands, is identical to the data backup procedure, except for the drive designators. Note that, because SET SAFETY OFF was included in the initialization program (smis.prg), error messages for "file already exists" will not be displayed.

```
COPY FILE A:ORDR.DBF TO ORDR.DBF>NUL
COPY FILE A:INVE.DBF TO INVE.DBF>NUL
COPY FILE A:SALE.DBF TO SALE.DBF>NUL
COPY FILE A:CUST.DBF TO CUST.DBF>NUL
COPY FILE A:PASSWORD.DBF TO PASSWORD.DBF>NUL
```

Upon completion of backup installation, the databases are indexed (i_data.prg):

```
DO i_data
SET CONSOLE ON
@ 5,0 CLEAR
RETURN
* End of r_data.prg
```

INDEXING DATABASES

In the event that an index file becomes corrupted for whatever reason, the user is allowed to recreate the index files from the data backup menu. Indexing is automatically done after the installation of backup data, using the following program.

```
* Program . . . . . . . . . . i_data.prg
* Description . . . . . . . . . . Database File Index
SET COLOR TO W+
    @ 5,0 CLEAR
    @ 3,25 SAY SPACE(30)
    @ 3,36 SAY "INDEXING"
SET COLOR TO W+*
    @22,26 SAY "P l e a s e  W a i t . . ."
SET COLOR TO W
USE ORDR
INDEX ON ORDRNR TO ORDR1
USE INVE
INDEX ON ITEMNR TO INVE1
USE SALE
INDEX ON SALECODE TO SALE1
USE CUST
INDEX ON CUSTCODE TO CUST1
USE PASSWORD
INDEX ON PASSWORD TO PASSWORD
USE
@ 5,0 CLEAR
RETURN
* End of i_data.prg
```

Chapter 8

User Help

Most commercial software programs dedicate the Function-One (F1) key to user help. This help might consist of a menu, text, or some kind of lookup function. Nantucket has provided Clipper with a built-in help function that, predictably, is activated by pressing the Function-One (F1) key.

THE [F1] HELP FEATURE

During normal operation of a Clipper-compiled program, pressing the F1 key during any GET, WAIT, MENU TO, or other variable entry routine will activate the help procedure. Clipper looks for a program named help.prg and, if it is found, Clipper passes three parameters to that program. These parameters are: (1) the name of the calling program, (2) the line number of the calling program that is awaiting user entry, and (3) the name of the variable that is awaiting user entry. It is with these three parameters that a sophisticated help facility can be incorporated into any application program.

The Sales Management System example uses a very elaborate help scheme. User help, via F1, is available at any point during operation of the program. Although some of it might appear to be overkill, you never know who might be sitting at the console trying to use your program!

The SMIS help facility uses a main help program (help.prg) as well as various help subprograms (denoted with an h__ prefix.) The main program includes the "welcome" screen, help for the utility programs, look-up functions, and the code for calling the subprograms.

Each subprogram contains the help instructions for a corresponding SMIS menu. The program h__main.prg contains the help code for the main menu (m__main.prg); h__ordr.prg contains the code for m__ordr, and so on.

The parameters that are passed to the help program by the calling program must be identified at the start of help.prg. It doesn't matter what they are called, just as long as they are identified. The SMIS example uses the parameter name "prg" to represent the calling program, "line" to represent the calling program line number, and "mvar" to represent the variable awaiting user input.

The particular type of help that is made available to the user is based on the three passed parameters. This is known as *context-specific help.* Actually, in the SMIS help facility, only the calling program (prg) and entry variable (mvar) parameters are used to identify the proper help text. The line number (line) parameter is not used.

The SMIS help program (help.prg) begins by identifying the three passed parameters:

```
* Program . . . . . . . . . help.prg
* Description . . . . . . . . Main Help Program
PARAMETERS prg,line,mvar
```

It is necessary to prevent the help program from calling itself in case the user presses the F1 key during a help screen. This is known as *recursive calling*; it must be prevented in the main program as well as each subprogram, using the following check:

```
IF prg = "HELP" .OR. prg = "H__MAIN" .OR. prg = "H__CUST" .OR.;
  prg = "H__ORDR" .OR. prg = "H__INVE" .OR. prg = "H__SALE",;
  .OR.
  prg = "H__PASS" .OR. prg = "H__DATA"
   RETURN
ENDIF
```

All of the help code is enclosed in one big CASE function (DO CASE). The CASE function evaluates the passed parameters "prg" and/or "mvar" in order to pick out the proper help message or function.

The first help message is a welcome that is displayed when the user presses F1 during password entry. The calling program is smis.prg, which is the initialization program containing the password entry routine:

```
CASE prg = "SMIS"
```

Note that the identifying parameter, "SMIS," must be enclosed in quotation marks and must be capitalized.

Clipper contains a command called SAVE SCREEN, which allows an entire screen display to be stored in memory and later redisplayed with the command RESTORE SCREEN. This is the trick to easily displaying user help screens without worrying about having to recreate the calling program screen.

The procedure in the first SMIS example consists of saving the password-entry screen and then clearing the screen below the permanent heading. The activity name (help) is then displayed on line zero:

```
SAVE SCREEN
    @ 5,0 CLEAR
    @ 0,70 SAY "<help>"
```

The welcome message is enclosed in a large window. The initial message, "Welcome to SMIS," is displayed in bright video. The rest of the message is displayed in normal video (see Fig. 8-1). This is shown by the following code:

```
    @ 8,19,24,61 BOX mFRAME1
    @ 9,21 SAY "Welcome to SMIS . . . Sales Management "
SET COLOR TO W+
    @ 9,21 SAY "Welcome to SMIS"
SET COLOR TO W
```

Fig. 8-1. The introductory help screen 1.

```
                                                          <help>
  +------------------------------------------------+
  |     Sales Management Information System         |
  |               PASSWORD ENTRY                    |
  +------------------------------------------------+



       +------------------------------------------+
       | Welcome to SMIS  ...  Sales Management   |
       | Information System. This software will   |
       | make it easy to track your customers,    |
       | orders, and sales. It is based on the    |
       | latest database techniques and has       |
       | been developed by software specialists.  |
       | SMIS is totally menu-driven, meaning     |
       | that each activity is accessed by        |
       | selection of a menu choice. Menu         |
       | choices are scrolled by using the up     |
       | arrow, down arrow, left arrow, and       |
       | right arrow keys. A selection is made    |
       | by pressing the Enter key.               |
       |                                          |
       |     Press any key to continue ...        |
       +------------------------------------------+
```

```
                                                              <help>

        ┌────────────────────────────────────────────────┐
        │   Sales Management Information System          │
        │              PASSWORD ENTRY                    │
        └────────────────────────────────────────────────┘



        ┌────────────────────────────────────────────────┐
        │   Remember, press [F1] if you need more        │
        │   information about any particular             │
        │   selection. If this is the first use of       │
        │   SMIS, system passwords have yet to be        │
        │   assigned. Therefore, at Password Entry,      │
        │   just type SMIS to get started.               │
        │                                                │
        │   Press any key to continue ...                │
        └────────────────────────────────────────────────┘
```

Fig. 8-2. The introductory help screen 2.

```
@10,21 SAY "Information System. This software will    "
@11,21 SAY "make it easy to track your customers,     "
@12,21 SAY "orders, and sales. It is based on the     "
@13,21 SAY "the latest database techniques and has    "
@14,21 SAY "been developed by software specialists.   "
@15,21 SAY "SMIS is totally menu-driven, meaning      "
@16,21 SAY "that each activity is accessed by         "
@17,21 SAY "selection of a menu choice. Menu          "
@18,21 SAY "choices are scrolled by using the up      "
@19,21 SAY "arrow, down arrow, left arrow, and        "
@20,21 SAY "right arrow keys. A selection is made     "
@21,21 SAY "by pressing the Enter key.                "
@23,25 SAY "Press any key to continue . . .           "
```

The first screen is displayed for 15 seconds, or until the user presses any key. The screen is then cleared, and a second screen of introductory information is displayed (see Fig. 8-2). The code to accomplish this is shown below:

```
? INKEY(15)
    @ 5,0 CLEAR
    @ 8,19,17,61 BOX mFRAME1
    @ 9,21 SAY "Remember, press [F1] if you need more     "
    @10,21 SAY "information about any particular          "
    @11,21 SAY "selection. If this is the first use of    "
    @12,21 SAY "SMIS, system passwords have yet to be     "
```

```
@13,21 SAY "assigned. Therefore, at Password Entry,        "
@14,21 SAY "just type SMIS to get started.                 "
@16,25 SAY "Press any key to continue . . .                "
```

The second screen is also displayed for 15 seconds, or until the user presses any key. The password entry screen, which was saved in memory with the SAVE SCREEN command, is redisplayed with the RESTORE SCREEN command:

```
? INKEY(15)
RESTORE SCREEN
RETURN
```

MENU HELP

If help (F1) is called from the main menu, then the variable that is passed is the menu memvar called "main." The line number and program name are not significant, because the "main" memvar is not used in any other program.

The help information for the main menu is contained in a separate subprogram called h_main.prg. This subprogram is called by the main help program (help.prg) and also has the menu variable "main" passed to it. Note, in the following segment of code, that again the main menu screen is first saved with the Clipper SAVE SCREEN command and then later restored with RESTORE SCREEN.

```
CASE mvar = "MAIN"
     SAVE SCREEN
          @ 5,0 CLEAR
          @ 0,70 SAY "<help>"
     DO h_main WITH main
     RESTORE SCREEN
     RETURN
```

The subprogram h_main.prg contains the help messages for main menu. The passed parameter "main" must be identified with the PARAMETERS function. The CASE command is used to display a message according to the value of "main" when the user pressed the F1 key from the main menu.

If the main menu position was the customer menu, then the value of main is one, and a help text about the customer menu is displayed using the following code (see Fig. 8-3):

```
* Program . . . . . . . . . . h_main.prg
* Description . . . . . . . . Main Menu Help
PARAMETERS main
```

68

```
                                                        <help>

              ┌────────────────────────────────────────┐
              │   Sales Management Information System   │
              │              MAIN MENU                  │
              └────────────────────────────────────────┘


              ┌──────────────────────────────────────────┐
              │  The Customer Menu allows you to:         │
              │                                           │
              │   1. Enter a new customer                 │
              │   2. Change or delete a customer          │
              │   3. List customers                       │
              │                                           │
              │  Press any key to continue ...            │
              └──────────────────────────────────────────┘
```

Fig. 8-3. The main menu help
screen.

```
DO CASE
   CASE main = 1
        @ 8,18,16,62 BOX mFRAME1
      SET COLOR TO W+
        @ 9,20 SAY "The Customer Menu allows you to:"
      SET COLOR TO W
        @11,20 SAY " 1. Enter a new customer"
        @12,20 SAY " 2. Change or delete a customer"
        @13,20 SAY " 3. List customers"
        @15,20 SAY "Press any key to continue . . . "
```

Similarly, for the other main menu choices, a help text can be
displayed according to the menu position at the time the user pressed
the F1 key:

```
   CASE main = 2
        @ 8,18,16,62 BOX mFRAME1
      SET COLOR TO W+
        @ 9,20 SAY "The Orders Menu allows you to:"
      SET COLOR TO W
        @11,20 SAY " 1. Enter a new order"
        @12,20 SAY " 2. Change or delete an order"
        @13,20 SAY " 3. List orders"
        @15,20 SAY "Press any key to continue . . . "
   CASE main = 3
        @ 8,18,16,62 BOX mFRAME1
```

```
          SET COLOR TO W+
               @ 9,20 SAY "The Inventory Menu allows you to:"
          SET COLOR TO W
               @11,20 SAY " 1. Enter a new item"
               @12,20 SAY " 2. Change or delete an item"
               @13,20 SAY " 3. List inventory"
               @15,20 SAY "Press any key to continue . . . "
     CASE main = 4
               @ 8,18,16,62 BOX mFRAME1
          SET COLOR TO W+
               @ 9,20 SAY "The Salesperson Menu allows you to:"
          SET COLOR TO W
               @11,20 SAY " 1. Enter a new salesperson"
               @12,20 SAY " 2. Change or delete a salesperson"
               @13,20 SAY " 3. List salespersons"
               @15,20 SAY "Press any key to continue . . . "
     CASE main = 5
               @ 8,18,16,62 BOX mFRAME1
          SET COLOR TO W+
               @ 9,20 SAY "The Password Menu allows you to:"
          SET COLOR TO W
               @11,20 SAY " 1. Enter a new password"
               @12,20 SAY " 2. Change or delete a password"
               @13,20 SAY " 3. List passwords"
               @15,20 SAY "Press any key to continue . . . "
     CASE main = 6
               @ 8,18,16,62 BOX mFRAME1
          SET COLOR TO W+
               @ 9,20 SAY "The Data Backup Menu allows you to:"
          SET COLOR TO W
               @11,20 SAY "1. Backup data to diskette"
               @12,20 SAY "2. Recall data from diskette"
               @13,20 SAY "3. Index databases"
               @15,20 SAY "Press any key to continue . . . "
     CASE main = 7
               @ 8,18,15,62 BOX mFRAME1
          SET COLOR TO W+
               @ 9,20 SAY "Return:"
          SET COLOR TO W
               @11,20 SAY "Returns SMIS to the password entry"
               @12,20 SAY "screen."
               @14,20 SAY "Press any key to continue . . . "
     CASE main = 8
               @ 8,18,14,62 BOX mFRAME1
          SET COLOR TO W+
               @ 9,20 SAY "Quit:"
          SET COLOR TO W
               @11,20 SAY "Quit and return to the DOS prompt."
               @13,20 SAY "Press any key to continue . . . "
ENDCASE
```

A message is displayed for 15 seconds, or until the user presses any key. The main menu help program then returns to the main help program:

```
? INKEY(15)
RETURN
* End of h__main.prg
```

The help technique for the orders menu of the Sales Management example is different, because that menu contains a submenu. That menu also contains two menu memvars, called "ordr1" and "ordr2." The main help program passes both of these variables, and the subprogram (h__ordr.prg) accommodates each menu variable value, as shown below:

```
CASE mvar = "ORDR"
    SAVE SCREEN
    @ 5,0 CLEAR
    @ 0,70 SAY "<help>"
    DO h__ordr WITH ordr1, ordr2
    RESTORE SCREEN
    RETURN
```

Recall, from the discussion of the main orders menu, that the menu variable "ordr2" was set to a value of nine as long as the submenu was not displayed on the screen. The orders menu help program, which follows, uses the values of both "ordr1" and "ordr2" to determine which message should be displayed, according to the menu position when the user pressed the F1 key:

```
* Program . . . . . . . . . . h__ordr.prg
* Description . . . . . . . . Orders Menu Help

PARAMETERS ordr1, ordr2
DO CASE
    CASE ordr1 = 1 .AND. ordr2 = 9
            @ 8,18,21,62 BOX mFRAME1
        SET COLOR TO W+
            @ 9,20 SAY "Enter:"
        SET COLOR TO W
            @11,20 SAY "A new order is added to the customer"
            @12,20 SAY "file. Order information includes:"
            @13,20 SAY " 1. Order Number"
            @14,20 SAY " 2. Customer Code"
            @15,20 SAY " 3. Salesperson Code"
            @16,20 SAY " 4. Quantity"
            @17,20 SAY " 5. Item Number"
            @18,20 SAY " 6. Order Date"
            @20,20 SAY "Press any key to continue . . . "
```

71

```
CASE ordr1 = 2 .AND. ordr2 = 9
        @ 8,18,19,62 BOX mFRAME1
    SET COLOR TO W+
        @ 9,20 SAY "Change or Delete:"
    SET COLOR TO W
        @11,20 SAY "An order may be changed or deleted."
        @12,20 SAY "First, the order number must be"
        @13,20 SAY "entered. Order information, except for"
        @14,20 SAY "the order number, may be changed. If"
        @15,20 SAY "an order is deleted, it may never be"
        @16,20 SAY "recalled."
        @18,20 SAY "Press any key to continue . . . "
CASE ordr1 = 3 .AND. ordr2 = 9
        @ 8,18,19,62 BOX mFRAME1
    SET COLOR TO W+
        @ 9,20 SAY "List:"
    SET COLOR TO W
        @11,20 SAY "Orders may be listed per selected"
        @12,20 SAY "criteria. Orders may be listed per:"
        @13,20 SAY " 1. All orders"
        @14,20 SAY " 2. Selected Customer Code"
        @15,20 SAY " 3. Selected Item Number"
        @16,20 SAY " 4. Selected Salesperson Code"
        @18,20 SAY "Press any key to continue . . . "
CASE ordr1 = 4 .AND. ordr2 = 9
        @ 8,18,14,62 BOX mFRAME1
    SET COLOR TO W+
        @9,20 SAY "Return:"
    SET COLOR TO W
        @11,20 SAY "Returns DEMO to the Main Menu."
        @13,20 SAY "Press any key to continue . . . "
```

The remaining messages correspond to the orders submenu for listing criteria. The menu memvar "ordr2" is the determining variable:

```
CASE ordr2 = 1
        @ 8,18,15,62 BOX mFRAME1
    SET COLOR TO W+
        @ 9,20 SAY "All Orders:"
    SET COLOR TO W
        @11,20 SAY "All orders will be displayed. The"
        @12,20 SAY "listing may also be printed out."
        @14,20 SAY "Press any key to continue . . . "
CASE ordr2 = 2
        @ 8,18,17,62 BOX mFRAME1
    SET COLOR TO W+
        @ 9,20 SAY "Customer Select:"
    SET COLOR TO W
        @11,20 SAY "You must enter a valid customer code."
        @12,20 SAY "Orders for that customer only will be"
```

```
                    @13,20 SAY "displayed. The listing may also be"
                    @14,20 SAY "printed out."
                    @16,20 SAY "Press any key to continue . . . "
           CASE ordr2 = 3
                    @ 8,18,17,62 BOX mFRAME1
              SET COLOR TO W+
                    @ 9,20 SAY "Item Number Select:"
              SET COLOR TO W
                    @11,20 SAY "You must enter a valid item number."
                    @12,20 SAY "Orders for that item only will be"
                    @13,20 SAY "displayed. The listing may also be"
                    @14,20 SAY "printed out."
                    @16,20 SAY "Press any key to continue . . . "
           CASE ordr2 = 4
                    @ 8,18,17,62 BOX mFRAME1
              SET COLOR TO W+
                    @ 9,20 SAY "Salesperson Select:"
              SET COLOR TO W
                    @11,20 SAY "You must enter a valid salesperson."
                    @12,20 SAY "Orders for that salesperson only will"
                    @13,20 SAY "be displayed. The listing may also be"
                    @14,20 SAY "printed out."
                    @16,20 SAY "Press any key to continue . . . "
           CASE ordr2 = 5
                    @ 8,18,14,62 BOX mFRAME1
              SET COLOR TO W+
                    @ 9,20 SAY "Return:"
              SET COLOR TO W
                    @11,20 SAY "Returns SMIS to the Orders Menu."
                    @13,20 SAY "Press any key to continue . . . "
     ENDCASE
     ? INKEY(15)
     RETURN
     * End of h__ordr.prg
```

Each of the other menus has a help procedure similar to that of the main menu help program. The full source code is included in Appendix A.

The main help program (help.prg) also includes help messages for each of the utility menu programs. The utility programs for listing (u__list.prg), data entry (u__entr.prg), data change (u__chng.prg), and data update (u__upda.prg) all have help messages. Each utility passes the program name, the memvar (mCHOICE), and the line number whenever the user presses the F1 key during a displayed utility.

The utility u__list.prg is identified in the main help program by the passed variable "prg," and then evaluated by the value of "mCHOICE," using the following code, to determine which help message is displayed:

```
CASE prg = "U__LIST"
    SAVE SCREEN
        @ 5,0 CLEAR
        @ 0,70 SAY "<help>"
    DO CASE
    CASE mCHOICE = 1
            @ 8,18,15,62 BOX mFRAME1
        SET COLOR TO W+
            @ 9,20 SAY "Forward:"
        SET COLOR TO W
            @11,20 SAY "To list the next page of"
            @12,20 SAY "information"
            @14,20 SAY "Press any key to continue . . ."
    CASE mCHOICE = 2
        @ 8,18,15,62 BOX mFRAME1
        @ 9,20 SAY "Backward:"
        @11,20 SAY "To list the previous page of"
        @12,20 SAY "information"
        @14,20 SAY "Press any key to continue . . ."
    CASE mCHOICE = 3
            @ 8,18,14,62 BOX mFRAME1
        SET COLOR TO W+
            @ 9,20 SAY "Top:"
        SET COLOR TO W
            @11,20 SAY "To list at the top of the file"
            @13,20 SAY "Press any key to continue . . ."
    CASE mCHOICE = 4
            @ 8,18,14,62 BOX mFRAME1
        SET COLOR TO W+
            @ 9,20 SAY "End:"
        SET COLOR TO W
            @11,20 SAY "To list at the end of the file"
            @13,20 SAY "Press any key to continue . . ."
    CASE mCHOICE = 5
            @ 8,18,14,62 BOX mFRAME1
        SET COLOR TO W+
            @ 9,20 SAY "Print:"
        SET COLOR TO W
            @11,20 SAY "To print the listing information"
            @13,20 SAY "Press any key to continue . . ."
    CASE mCHOICE = 6
            @ 8,18,14,62 BOX mFRAME1
        SET COLOR TO W+
            @ 9,20 SAY "Return:"
        SET COLOR TO W
            @11,20 SAY "Returns SMIS to the previous menu."
            @13,20 SAY "Press any key to continue . . ."
    ENDCASE
    ? INKEY(15)
    RESTORE SCREEN
    RETURN
```

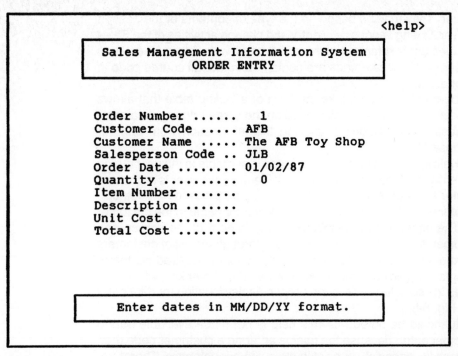

```
                                              <help>

        ┌──────────────────────────────────────────┐
        │    Sales Management Information System    │
        │               ORDER ENTRY                 │
        └──────────────────────────────────────────┘


          Order Number ......    1
          Customer Code .....  AFB
          Customer Name .....  The AFB Toy Shop
          Salesperson Code ..  JLB
          Order Date ........  01/02/87
          Quantity ..........    0
          Item Number .......
          Description .......
          Unit Cost .........
          Total Cost ........



        ┌──────────────────────────────────────────┐
        │     Enter dates in MM/DD/YY format.       │
        └──────────────────────────────────────────┘
```

Fig. 8-4. The date type help screen.

The other utility help programs are structured in a similar manner, as shown in the Appendix A source code.

DATA ENTRY HELP

Help messages can also be displayed during user entry of database information. In the SMIS example application, a help message is displayed when the user presses the F1 key during entry of a date. This message is based on the type of memvar that is passed from the calling program. Using the Clipper TYPE( ) function, the passed variable is tested for date type. For all date-type memvars, regardless of the program that help is called from, the date help message is displayed using the code shown below. Note that the screen is not cleared. The one-line help message is displayed at the bottom of the screen for five seconds, or until the user presses any key (see Fig. 8-4):

```
CASE TYPE(mvar) = "D"
    @20,0 CLEAR
    @21,23,23,57 BOX mFRAME1
    @22,25 SAY "Enter dates in MM/DD/YY format."
    ? INKEY(5)
    @20,0 CLEAR
    RETURN
```

Other single-line help messages can be displayed in a similar manner. They may be based on the type of contents of the passed memvar. During various data entry and change activities of the Sales Management example, address information is requested. Help messages for these entries are contained in the full source code in Appendix A.

User help can also take the form of a *lookup table* that allows the user to have choices displayed on the screen during data entry activities. This includes displaying the information from another database file.

Help for looking up customer codes is available to the user during data entry, change, or list activities. Whenever the user is requested to enter a customer code, the F1 key may be pressed to "look up" the desired code and corresponding customer name in the customer file. The information is displayed at the bottom of the screen one customer at a time, and the user scrolls through the list of customers with the up-arrow and down-arrow keys until the desired customer is displayed. The customer is selected with the Enter key, which also places the selected code in the proper display location for data entry (see Fig. 8-5).

It should be noted that this help is not made available during customer entry, because the user is entering a customer code that, supposedly, does not yet exist in the customer database. Therefore, help is determined by the passed memvar "MCUSTCODE" in any calling program except for the customer entry program.

Fig. 8-5. The customer code help screen.

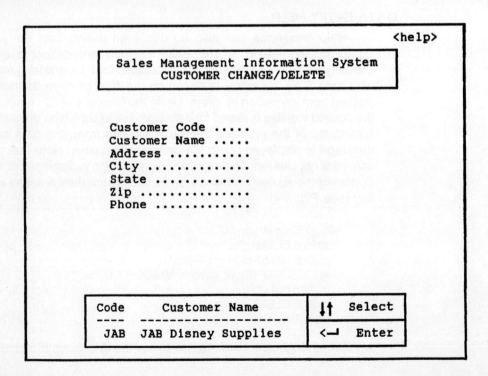

The lookup information is displayed, using the following sequence of commands, in a window that displays the customer code and name as the user scrolls with the up- and down-arrow keys. The user may also use the PgUp and PgDn keys to scroll in groups of 10 customers, and the Home and End keys to display the first and the last customer in the customer file.

```
CASE mvar = "MCUSTCODE" .AND. prg != "E__CUST"
    @20,0 CLEAR
    @20,19,24,61 BOX mFRAME1
    @21,21 SAY "Code   Customer Name   "
    @22,21 SAY "----  --------------------"
    @20,48 SAY CHR(194)
    @21,48 SAY CHR(179)
    @22,48 SAY CHR(195)
    @22,49 SAY REPLICATE(CHR(196),13)
    @22,61 SAY CHR(180)
    @23,48 SAY CHR(179)
    @24,48 SAY CHR(193)
    @21,50 SAY CHR(025)+CHR(024)+" Select"
    @23,50 SAY CHR(017)+CHR(196)+CHR(217)+ " Enter"
```

If the user has already entered a customer code, as is the case during customer information change/delete, then the help window will begin displaying the customer code and name at that entered code:

```
USE CUST INDEX CUST1
SEEK mCUSTCODE
IF ! FOUND()
    GO TOP
ENDIF
DO WHILE .T.
    SET COLOR TO W+
        @23,22 SAY CUSTCODE+" "+CUSTNAME
    SET COLOR TO W
```

The INKEY() function returns the ASCII value of the keypress. Each allowable key is checked, but only the Enter key permits a return to the calling program:

```
C=0
DO WHILE C=0
    C=INKEY()
ENDDO
IF C=13                            && ENTER key
    STORE UPPER(CUSTCODE) TO mCUSTCODE
    EXIT
ENDIF
IF C=5                             && Up Arrow key
```

```
            SKIP -1
        IF BOF( )
             GO BOTTOM
        ENDIF
    ENDIF
    IF C = 24                    && Dn Arrow key
        SKIP
        IF EOF( )
             GO TOP
        ENDIF
    ENDIF
    IF C = 18                    && PgUp key
        SKIP -10
        IF BOF( )
             GO BOTTOM
        ENDIF
    ENDIF
    IF C = 3                     && PgDn key
        SKIP 10
        IF EOF( )
             GO TOP
        ENDIF
    ENDIF
    IF C = 1                     && Home key
        GO TOP
    ENDIF
    IF C = 6                     && End key
        GO BOTTOM
    ENDIF
    LOOP
ENDDO
CLOSE DATABASES
@20,0 CLEAR
RETURN
```

Lookup help is available for other user entry data in the Sales
Management example, including order number, as shown in the
following code. During order number help, the user may scroll
through the orders file (ORDR.DBF) while help displays the order
number, customer code, salesperson code, and date of the order
(see Fig. 8-6).

```
CASE mvar = "MORDRNR" .AND. prg ! = "E__ODRD"
    @20,0 CLEAR
    @19,24,61 BOX mFRAME1
    @21,21 SAY "Ordr  Cust  Sale    Date  "
    @22,21 SAY "----  ----  ----  --------"
```

```
                                                    <help>
        ┌─────────────────────────────────────────┐
        │    Sales Management Information System   │
        │            ORDER CHANGE/DELETE           │
        └─────────────────────────────────────────┘


            Order Number ......
            Customer Code .....
            Customer Name .....
            Salesperson Code ..
            Order Date ........
            Quantity ..........
            Item Number .......
            Description .......
            Unit Cost .........
            Total Cost ........


        ┌──────────────────────────────┬──────────────┐
        │  Ordr   Cust  Sale    Date   │ ↓↑   Select  │
        │  ────   ────  ────  ──────── │              │
        │    1    JAB   JLB   01/02/87 │ <┘   Enter   │
        └──────────────────────────────┴──────────────┘
```

Fig. 8-6. The order number
help screen.

```
@20,48 SAY CHR(194)
@21,48 SAY CHR(179)
@22,48 SAY CHR(195)
@22,49 SAY REPLICATE(CHR(196),13)
@22,61 SAY CHR(180)
@23,48 SAY CHR(179)
@24,48 SAY CHR(193)
@21,50 SAY CHR(025)+CHR(024)+"   Select"
@23,50 SAY CHR(017)+CHR(196)+CHR(217)+ " Enter"
USE ORDR INDEX ORDR1
SEEK mORDRNR
IF ! FOUND( )
    GO TOP
ENDIF
```

The order number (ORDRNR), customer code (CUSTCODE), and salesperson code (SALECODE) are character variables; however, the date (DATE) is not. Because the displayed help line is, in effect, the sum of the four displayed fields, the date variable (DATE) must be converted to a character variable using the DTOC (date to character) function:

```
DO WHILE .T.
    SET COLOR TO W+
        @23,22 SAY ORDRNR+" "+CUSTCODE+" "+SALECODE+;
```

```
                 "     " + DTOC(DATE)
         SET COLOR TO W
         C = 0
         DO WHILE C = 0
            C = INKEY( )
         ENDDO
         IF C = 13                        && ENTER key
            STORE ORDRNR TO mORDRNR
            EXIT
         ENDIF
         IF C = 5                         && Up Arrow key
           SKIP -1
           IF BOF( )
              GO BOTTOM
           ENDIF
         ENDIF
         IF C = 24                        && Dn Arrow key
           SKIP
           IF EOF( )
              GO TOP
           ENDIF
         ENDIF
         IF C = 18                        && PgUp key
           SKIP -10
           IF BOF( )
              GO BOTTOM
           ENDIF
         ENDIF
         IF C = 3                         && PgDn key
           SKIP 10
           IF EOF( )
              GO TOP
           ENDIF
         ENDIF
         IF C = 1                         && Home key
           GO TOP
         ENDIF
         IF C = 6                         && End key
           GO BOTTOM
         ENDIF
         LOOP
      ENDDO
      CLOSE DATABASES
      @20,0 CLEAR
      RETURN
```

There might be some instances when help is not made available
to the user. It is a good idea, in such cases, to display a message
to that effect. The CASE evaluation of the main help program can
be concluded by using OTHERWISE, as shown below, to cover all

situations in which help is called but not included in the help procedure.

```
    OTHERWISE
        SAVE SCREEN
        @20,0 CLEAR
        @22,27,24,52 BOX mFRAME1
        @23,29 SAY "Help is not available!"
        ? INKEY(5)
        @20,0 CLEAR
        RESTORE SCREEN
        RETURN
ENDCASE
RETURN
* End of help.prg
```

Chapter 9

User-Defined Functions

A unique and very exciting aspect of Clipper is its ability to call external functions with passed parameters. This opens the door for programmers to develop their own library of additional functions for use in their own applications. This chapter will examine the Clipper *user-defined function* (UDF), create some examples, and show how these examples can be used within an application.

THE DEFINITION OF UDF

Dozens of functions already exist in the dBASE language, such as EOF( ) for end-of-file and STR( ) for numeric-to-character conversion. Others have been added by Clipper, such as VALID for data validation.

Additional functions have been included on the Clipper distribution diskettes in the form of an extended library. This extended library consists of functions written in dBASE, C, and 8086 assembly language. These functions may be used just like the built-in dBASE and Clipper functions. Furthermore, using the same principles, tailor-made (user-defined) functions can be generated.

A simple UDF can be written in dBASE, compiled with Clipper, and linked as a separate object-code file. A series of UDFs can even be included in a single compiled file. The extended library on the Clipper diskettes, for example, includes the source-code programs and the object files for three libraries, each of which contains several functions.

Several software companies sell UDF packages that contain various additional functions that can be compiled and linked with Clipper applications. Other UDFs have been placed in the public domain and can be found in database magazines.

UDF CREATION

Suppose that it is necessary to continually calculate the percentage increase in a particular application. The following program code would have to be repeated for every calculation.

```
STORE 1000 TO pres_val
STORE 1100 TO next_val
STORE (next_val-pres_val)/pres_val * 100 TO incr_pct
? incr_pct
```

A user-defined function can be created to automatically do the percentage increase calculation whenever that function is called.

The function will be named PCT( ). The parameters pres_val and next_val must be defined whenever PCT( ) is called. The UDF will return the value incr_pct. The new function, shown below, is called just like any other dBASE or Clipper function.

```
STORE 1000 TO pres_val
STORE 1100 TO next_val
STORE PCT(pres_val,next_val) TO incr_pct
? incr_pct
```

Although the amount of code generated in this example is about the same for both methods, in a lengthy calculation, there could be a quite significant reduction by using a UDF.

The UDF PCT( ) is included in a file named myfuncts.prg, which may include other dBASE functions. The parameters must be identified, and the percentage increase is returned:

```
* Program . . . . . . . . . myfuncts.prg
* Description . . . . . . . . User Defined Functions
FUNCTION PCT
PARAMETERS pres_val, next_val
RETURN ( (next_val-pres_val)/pres_val*100)
* End of my functs.prg
```

UDF VALIDATION

A more powerful use of the UDF is in data entry validation. A special function may even be designed to look up entered data in a database file as a means of verifying a correct user entry.

In the Sales Management Information example, the orders-change program (c_ordr.prg) validated the entered order number by looking it up in the orders file. A UDF can be used to accomplish the same task and will usually reduce the amount of program code required.

The UDF name is F_ORDR, and the parameter that is passed is the order number memvar, mORDRNR. The UDF is called by the Clipper VALID function and returns a logical true (.T.) if the entry is acceptable, as shown in the following code.

```
* Program . . . . . . . . . c_ordr.prg (partial)
* Description . . . . . . . . Order Change/Delete (using UDFs)
DO WHILE .T.
    SET COLOR TO W+
        @ 7,20 SAY "Order Number . . . . ."
    SET COLOR TO W
        @22,31 SAY "Press [F1] for Help."
        @24,26 SAY "Leave blank to return to menu."
        @ 7,40 GET mORDRNR PICTURE "###";
            VALID F_ORDR(mORDRNR)
    READ
        @22,0 CLEAR
        @ 7,20 SAY "Order Number . . . . . ."
    STORE STR(VAL(mORDRNR),3) TO mORDRNR
    SET COLOR TO /W
        @ 7,40 SAY mORDRNR
    SET COLOR TO W
```

The UDF is included in myfuncts.prg and is identified by the FUNCTION command. The passed parameter must be identified in the PARAMETERS command. The VALID logic memvar that is returned by the UDF is called my_udf. This memvar must be identified in each RETURN command.

A blank order number is allowed during entry as a means of returning the user to the previous menu. Therefore, an EMPTY(mORDRNR) sets the UDF memvar my_udf to a logical true (.T.).

The order number (mORDRNR) is looked up in the orders file (ORDR.DBF). If it is not found, an error message is displayed by the UDF, and a logical false (.F.) is returned to the orders change program. If the order number is valid, a logical true (.T.) is returned, and order number entry is completed. This is shown in the following code.

```
* Program . . . . . . . . . myfuncts.prg
* Description . . . . . . User Defined Functions
FUNCTION F_ORDR   && validates entered order number
PARAMETERS mORDRNR
```

```
STORE STR(VAL(mORDRNR),3) TO mORDRNR
STORE .F. TO my__udf
IF EMPTY(mORDRNR)
    STORE .T. TO my__udf
    RETURN (my__udf)
ENDIF
USE ORDR INDEX ORDR1
SEEK mORDRNR
IF FOUND( )
    STORE .T. TO my__udf
ELSE
    STORE .F. TO my__udf
    SAVE SCREEN
        @20,0 CLEAR
        ? CHR(7)
        SET COLOR TO W+*
            @22,29 SAY "Order Number not found!"
        SET COLOR TO W
    ? INKEY(10)
    RESTORE SCREEN
ENDIF
USE
RETURN (my__udf)
```

A UDF can also be used in entry validation to display derived information. During the order information change procedure of c__ordr.prg, the user enters an item number from the inventory file, and the item description, unit cost, and total cost (the unit cost multiplied by the quantity) are displayed.

The UDF method consists of displaying the item information during the UDF validation. The user-defined function is named F__ITEM, which is called by the VALID function and is passed the item number memvar (mITEMNR) and the quantity (mQTY):

```
SET COLOR TO W+
    @13,20 SAY "Item Number . . . . . . ."
SET COLOR TO W
    @22,31 SAY "Press [F1] for Help."
    @13,40 GET mITEMNR PICTURE "###";
        VALID F__ITEM(mITEMNR,mQTY)
READ
    @22,0 CLEAR
    @13,20 SAY "Item Number . . . . . . ."
STORE STR(VAL(mITEMNR),3) TO mITEMNR
SET COLOR TO /W
    @13,40 SAY mITEMNR
SET COLOR TO W
```

The UDF F__ITEM does not allow a blank entry. If a valid item number is entered, the description and unit cost are displayed. The total cost can be calculated, because the quantity memvar (mQTY) was passed to the UDF along with the entry memvar (mITEMNR). This UDF is shown below.

```
FUNCTION F__ITEM   && validates entered item number
PARAMETERS mITEMNR,mQTY
STORE STR(VAL(mITEMNR),3) TO mITEMNR
STORE .F. TO my__udf
IF EMPTY(mITEMNR)
    STORE .F. TO my__udf
    RETURN (my__udf)
ENDIF
USE INVE INDEX INVE1
SEEK mITEMNR
IF FOUND( )
    STORE .T. TO my__udf
    SET COLOR TO /W
        @14,40 SAY DESC
        @15,40 SAY TRANSFORM(COST,"###,###.##")
        @16,40 SAY TRANSFORM(COST*mQTY,"###,###.##")
    SET COLOR TO W
ELSE
    STORE .F. TO my__udf
    SAVE SCREEN
        @20,0 CLEAR
        ? CHR(7)
        SET COLOR TO W+*
            @22,29 SAY "Item Number not found!"
        SET COLOR TO W
    ? INKEY(10)
    RESTORE SCREEN
ENDIF
USE
RETURN (my__udf)
* End of myfuncts.prg
```

THE EXTEND FUNCTIONS

The EXTEND library that is included with Nantucket's Clipper contains many extra functions that can be used in a compiled application. Some of these UDFs were designed to help make Clipper more compatible with dBASE functions, while others are a true extension of the dBASE language.

The EXTEND functions, written by Tom Rettig and Brian Russell for Nantucket, are included in three separate object-code modules. EXTENDA.OBJ contains UDFs written in 8086 assembly language; EXTENDC.OBJ contains UDFs written in C; EXTENDDB.OBJ contains UDFs written in dBASE. The corresponding source code for each of these modules is included on the Clipper diskettes, along with full documentation.

The assembly language EXTEND library includes the printer-check UDF discussed in Chapter 6. If a printer is connected and online when the ISPRINTER( ) UDF is called, a logical true (.T.) is returned to the calling program.

The C version of the EXTEND library includes some additional functions that can be very useful when you are including data-backup-to-floppy-diskette routines for large databases. RECSIZE( ) returns the size in bytes of any database file, and DISKSPACE( ) returns the amount of empty space remaining on a disk. Another C function, LUPDATE( ), returns the date of the last database update, much as the same function in dBASE III does.

The dBASE version of the EXTEND library offers many UDFs that make Clipper functions equivalent to some of the newer dBASE III PLUS functions; these include MIN( ), MAX( ), LEFT( ), RIGHT( ), and others. Additional functions include the EMPTY( ) function that is used extensively throughout this book.

UDFs can substantially streamline an applications program, whether they are written in dBASE, C, or assembly language. The ideas discussed in this chapter only begin to show how UDFs may be used.

Chapter 10

Compiling With Clipper

The act of compiling a dBASE language program or series of programs can vary from one application to another. This chapter discusses how programs are typically compiled with Clipper, as well as how and why variations in compiling might come into play.

COMPILING PROGRAMS

Compiling a program results in the creation of an object-code file. This file can be linked with other object (.OBJ) and library (.LIB) files to produce an executable (.EXE) file.

The Clipper compiler creates an object-code file from dBASE program files. In the typical application, calling on Clipper to compile the highest-level program results in it and all of its subordinate programs being compiled automatically. For the SMIS example, compiling the initialization program (smis.prg) results in 34 program files being compiled into a single object-code file. (The help files must be compiled separately.)

Assuming that the Clipper compiler software and all of the SMIS programs are contained on the same drive (C:), the procedure for invoking the compiler from DOS is shown in Fig. 10-1.

Clipper provides some options concerning the object code. Including a "-n" at the end of the Clipper command line results in what is called *enhanced-native* object code, which will increase the

```
C> CLIPPER SMIS

The Clipper Compiler, Winter '85
Copyright (c) 1985, 1986 Nantucket Inc., All Rights Reserved

Compiling SMIS.PRG
Compiling M_MAIN.PRG
Compiling M_CUST.PRG
Compiling M_ORDR.PRG
Compiling M_INVE.PRG
Compiling M_SALE.PRG
Compiling M_PASS.PRG
Compiling M_DATA.PRG
Compiling E_CUST.PRG
Compiling C_CUST.PRG
Compiling L_CUST.PRG
Compiling E_ORDR.PRG
Compiling C_ORDR.PRG
Compiling L_ORDR.PRG
Compiling E_INVE.PRG
Compiling C_INVE.PRG
Compiling L_INVE.PRG
Compiling E_SALE.PRG
Compiling C_SALE.PRG
Compiling L_SALE.PRG
Compiling E_PASS.PRG
Compiling C_PASS.PRG
Compiling L_PASS.PRG
Compiling B_DATA.PRG
Compiling R_DATA.PRG
Compiling I_DATA.PRG
Compiling U_DENY.PRG
Compiling U_INFI.PRG
Compiling U_ENTR.PRG
Compiling U_NOFI.PRG
Compiling U_CHNG.PRG
Compiling U_SURE.PRG
Compiling U_UPDA.PRG
Compiling U_LIST.PRG
Code Size:29212    Symbols:2144    Constants:8224
```

Fig. 10-1. Compiling the SMIS example.

program's operating speed, but also increase the object-code size. Including a "-l" option removes the program source-code line numbers from the resultant object code, thereby reducing object code size. Including a "-s" option suppresses the actual object code creation, thereby offering a compilation test of the program code.

Use of the -1 option can be quite significant. The SMIS example application results in a SMIS.EXE file of 193,088 bytes after linking, as explained in detail in Chapter 11. Using the -1 option to remove the source-code line numbers results in a SMIS.EXE size of 182,256 bytes. This size reduction can be seen after compiling by comparing

```
C> CLIPPER SMIS

The Clipper Compiler, Winter '85
Copyright (c) 1985, 1986 Nantucket Inc., All Rights Reserved

Code Size:29212     Symbols:2144     Constants:8224


C> CLIPPER SMIS.PRG -1

The Clipper Compiler, Winter '85
Copyright (c) 1985, 1986 Nantucket Inc., All Rights Reserved

Code Size:21661     Symbols:2144     Constants:8206


C> CLIPPER HELP

The Clipper Compiler, Winter '85
Copyright (c) 1985, 1986 Nantucket Inc., All Rights Reserved

Code Size:14373     Symbols:624     Constants:10016


C> CLIPPER HELP.PRG -1

The Clipper Compiler, Winter '85
Copyright (c) 1985, 1986 Nantucket Inc., All Rights Reserved

Code Size:11073     Symbols:624     Constants:9968
```

Fig. 10-2. Compiling with the -1 Option.

```
C> COPY CON: PROG1.CLP

PROG_A
PROG_B
PROG_C
^Z

C> CLIPPER @ PROG1

The Clipper Compiler, Winter '85
Copyright (c) 1985, 1986 Nantucket Inc., All Rights Reserved

Compiling PROG_A.PRG
Compiling PROG_B.PRG
Compiling PROG_C.PRG
Code Size:1001     Symbols:134     Constants:724
```

Fig. 10-3. Compiling a clip file.

the code size values of normal compiling versus the Clipper -1 option (see Fig. 10-2).

Note that using any of the compile options requires that the full program name (including extension) be given, followed by a space, the dash (-) and the option in lowercase only. Failure to include the space between the program name and the option will cause the option to be ignored without warning.

Errors that occur during compiling are displayed as they occur. The Clipper user manual contains a glossary of error messages.

The Clipper user manual also discusses variations on compiling, such as breaking an application into groups of programs. Compiling programs in this way might be required for large applications or for the creation of overlays. This approach might also be useful during program debugging.

Compiling only groups of programs requires the creation of a *clip file*, which consists of a list of programs that are to be included in the compiled object-code file. The clip file (.CLP) can be created with a text editor or by using the DOS COPY CON command. The clip file is then compiled by using the Clipper command with the @ symbol to identify the .CLP file (see Fig. 10-3).

Breaking up an application into several object-code files requires a great deal of care in developing the program structure. The calling of programs by more than one object-code file can result in errors during linking.

COMPILING HELP PROGRAMS

Help programs must be compiled separately from the main application program. In the Sales Management Information example, the main help program (help.prg) also contains eight subprograms that will compile automatically (see Fig. 10-4), resulting in a HELP.OBJ object code file.

Fig. 10-4. Compiling the SMIS help file.

```
C> CLIPPER HELP

The Clipper Compiler, Winter '85
Copyright (c) 1985, 1986 Nantucket Inc., All Rights Reserved

Compiling HELP.PRG
Compiling H_MAIN.PRG
Compiling H_CUST.PRG
Compiling H_ORDR.PRG
Compiling H_INVE.PRG
Compiling H_SALE.PRG
Compiling H_PASS.PRG
Compiling H_DATA.PRG
Code Size:14373    Symbols:624    Constants:10016
```

COMPILING UDFs

Likewise, programs containing the UDFs must be compiled separately. Compiling the example UDF program (myfuncts.prg) in the previous chapter results in the object-code file MYFUNCTS.OBJ, which can then be linked with a main application file.

Chapter 11

Linking Files

Compiled (object code) files undergo one final procedure in order to produce a final executable program. This last task requires that the object code files be linked with the library files of the compiler. This chapter will discuss the methods of linking files to produce the final application program.

LINKING CODE

The result of compiling the SMIS example was the creation of two object code files. SMIS.OBJ includes all of the SMIS program files, and HELP.OBJ includes the help program files. These two object code files can be linked with the EXTENDA code and Clipper library by using the PLINK86 Linkage Editor that is included with Clipper.

The simplest method of linking involves using a DOS command, as shown in Fig. 11-1. This method assumes that the object code files, linkage editor, and Clipper library (CLIPPER.LIB) all reside on the same drive directory (C:). The executable file SMIS.EXE results from linking as shown. The number in parenthesis is the load module size in kilobytes. The actual amount of memory needed to run the final .EXE program must be increased approximately 64K because of the DOS and Clipper overhead memory.

Note that because a user-defined function, ISPRINTER( ), from

```
C> PLINK86 FI SMIS,HELP,EXTENDA

PSA Linkage Editor (Nantucket Clipper) version 1.46.c
Copyright (C) 1984 by Phoenix Software Associates Ltd.


SMIS.EXE  (180K)
```

Fig. 11-1. Simple linking of the SMIS example.

the assembly-code EXTEND file was used in SMIS, the EXTENDA object code must also be linked with the SMIS and HELP object-code files.

The PLINK86 linkage editor also includes an interactive method. This method might be useful when many different link commands are required in an application. This method of linking SMIS is shown in Fig. 11-2. The LIB command is optional, because the PSA Linkage Editor knows that the Clipper library is included. The OUTPUT command is also optional; it can be used to rename the resulting executable file.

RUNNING A CLIPPER PROGRAM

As in interpretive dBASE, the DOS system configuration must be modified for Clipper applications. Therefore, a CONFIG.SYS file should be included in the boot-up directory of the computer system incorporating a Clipper program. This file can be created with the DOS COPY CON command, as shown in Fig. 11-3.

The executable Clipper program and associated database and index files must reside in the same drive directory. The databases and indexes are created automatically in the SMIS application.

The SMIS program is started by typing SMIS at the DOS prompt.

```
C> PLINK86

PSA Linkage Editor (Nantucket Clipper) version 1.46.c
Copyright (C) 1984 by Phoenix Software Associates Ltd.

=>FILE SMIS
=>FILE HELP
=>FILE EXTENDA
=>LIB CLIPPER
=>OUTPUT SMIS
=>;


SMIS.EXE  (180K)
```

Fig. 11-2. Interactive linking of the SMIS example.

```
C> COPY CON: CONFIG.SYS

FILES=20
BUFFERS=15
^Z

        1 File(s) copied
```

Fig. 11-3. Creating the
CONGIG.SYS file.

SUMMARY

As you have seen, Clipper is a powerful tool for dBASE language applications programmers. This book has only touched some of the more basic techniques of compiled programming.

Clipper's parameter-passing ability with the user-defined function opens the door for programmers to develop custom applications with specially created dBASE language extensions. I hope that this book has helped stimulate that creativity.

Appendix A

SMIS Source Code

Appendix A contains the source code for the Sales Management Information System example application used throughout *Clipper: dBASE Compiler Applications.* The programs are presented in order of activity type as shown below.

u__upda.prg   u__nofi.prg
u__list.prg   u__deny.prg
u__infi.prg   u__sure.prg

SMIS.PRG

```
* Program .......... smis.prg
* Description ...... Initialization Program

SET CONFIRM ON
SET BELL OFF
SET DELETED ON
SET ESCAPE OFF

PUBLIC mPW
PUBLIC mAL
PUBLIC mCHOICE
PUBLIC mFRAME1
PUBLIC mFRAME2
PUBLIC mSURE

mFRAME1 = CHR(218)+CHR(196)+CHR(191)+CHR(179)+;
          CHR(217)+CHR(196)+CHR(192)+CHR(179)

CLEAR
SET COLOR TO W+
   @ 3,20 SAY " xxxxx     xxx     xxx    xxxxxxx    xxxxx "
   @ 4,20 SAY "xxxxxxx    xxxx   xxxx    xxxxxxx   xxxxxxx"
   @ 5,20 SAY "xxx        xxxxx xxxxx     xxx      xxx    "
   @ 6,20 SAY " xxx       xxx xxx xxx     xxx       xxx   "
   @ 7,20 SAY "  xxx      xxx  x  xxx     xxx        xxx  "
   @ 8,20 SAY "   xxx     xxx     xxx     xxx         xxx "
   @ 9,20 SAY "    xxx    xxx     xxx     xxx         xxx"
   @10,20 SAY "xxxxxxx    xxx     xxx    xxxxxxx   xxxxxxx"
   @11,20 SAY " xxxxx     xxx     xxx    xxxxxxx    xxxxx "
   @15,20,19,60 BOX mFRAME1
SET COLOR TO W
   @17,23 SAY "Sales Management Information System"
SET COLOR TO W+
   @22,22 SAY "Copyright (c) 1987 by: TAB BOOKS Inc."
SET COLOR TO W
   @23,22 SAY REPLICATE(CHR(196),37)
? INKEY(5)
CLEAR

SET COLOR TO W
   @ 1,10,4,69 BOX mFRAME1
   @ 2,23 SAY "Sales Management Information System"

IF ! FILE("ORDR.DBF")
   SET COLOR TO W+
      @ 3,25 SAY SPACE(30)
      @ 3,34 SAY "INSTALLATION"
   SET COLOR TO W  CREATE DUMMY
STORE "ORDRNR    C3  "  TO Field1
STORE "CUSTCODE  C3  "  TO Field2
STORE "SALECODE  C3  "  TO Field3
STORE "QTY       N4  "  TO Field4
STORE "ITEMNR    C3  "  TO Field5
STORE "DATE      D8  "  TO Field6
FOR F = 1 TO 6
   STORE STR(F,1) TO count
   APPEND BLANK
   STORE "Field" + count TO FN
```

97

```
      REPLACE field_name WITH SUBSTR(&FN,1,10)
      REPLACE field_type WITH SUBSTR(&FN,11,1)
      REPLACE field_len  WITH VAL(SUBSTR(&FN,12,2))
      REPLACE field_dec  WITH VAL(SUBSTR(&FN,14,1))
   NEXT
   CREATE ORDR FROM DUMMY
   INDEX ON ORDRNR TO ORDR1
   USE
      @ 7,25 SAY "ORDR.DBF is created and indexed"
   ERASE DUMMY.DBF

   CREATE DUMMY
   STORE "ITEMNR     C3  " TO Field1
   STORE "DESC       C20 " TO Field2
   STORE "COST       N8 2" TO Field3
   FOR F = 1 TO 3
      STORE STR(F,1) TO count
      APPEND BLANK
      STORE "Field" + count TO FN
      REPLACE field_name WITH SUBSTR(&FN,1,10)
      REPLACE field_type WITH SUBSTR(&FN,11,1)
      REPLACE field_len  WITH VAL(SUBSTR(&FN,12,2))
      REPLACE field_dec  WITH VAL(SUBSTR(&FN,14,1))
   NEXT
   CREATE INVE FROM DUMMY
   INDEX ON ITEMNR TO INVE1
   USE
      @ 9,25 SAY "INVE.DBF is created and indexed"
   ERASE DUMMY.DBF

   CREATE DUMMY
   STORE "SALECODE   C3  " TO Field1
   STORE "SALENAME   C20 " TO Field2
   STORE "ADDRESS    C20 " TO Field3
   STORE "CITY       C20 " TO Field4
   STORE "STATE      C2  " TO Field5
   STORE "ZIP        C5  " TO Field6
   STORE "PHONE      C12 " TO Field7
   STORE "AGE        N2  " TO Field8
   STORE "HIRED      D8  " TO Field9
   STORE "BASEPAY    N6 2" TO Field10
   FOR F = 1 TO 10
      IF F < 10
         STORE STR(F,1) TO count
      ELSE
         STORE STR(F,2) TO count
      ENDIF
      APPEND BLANK
      STORE "Field" + count TO FN
      REPLACE field_name WITH SUBSTR(&FN,1,10)
      REPLACE field_type WITH SUBSTR(&FN,11,1)
      REPLACE field_len  WITH VAL(SUBSTR(&FN,12,2))
      REPLACE field_dec  WITH VAL(SUBSTR(&FN,14,1))
   NEXT
   CREATE SALE FROM DUMMY
   INDEX ON SALECODE TO SALE1
   USE
      @11,25 SAY "SALE.DBF is created and indexed"
   ERASE DUMMY.DBF

   CREATE DUMMY
   STORE "CUSTCODE   C3  " TO Field1
   STORE "CUSTNAME   C20 " TO Field2
   STORE "ADDRESS    C20 " TO Field3
   STORE "CITY       C20 " TO Field4
   STORE "STATE      C2  " TO Field5
```

```
        STORE "ZIP         C5  " TO Field6
        STORE "PHONE       C12 " TO Field7
        FOR F = 1 TO 7
          STORE STR(F,1) TO count
          APPEND BLANK
          STORE "Field" + count TO FN
          REPLACE field_name WITH SUBSTR(&FN,1,10)
          REPLACE field_type WITH SUBSTR(&FN,11,1)
          REPLACE field_len  WITH VAL(SUBSTR(&FN,12,2))
          REPLACE field_dec  WITH VAL(SUBSTR(&FN,14,1))
        NEXT
        CREATE CUST FROM DUMMY
        INDEX ON CUSTCODE TO CUST1
        USE
          @13,25 SAY "CUST.DBF is created and indexed"
        ERASE DUMMY.DBF

        CREATE DUMMY
        STORE "PASSWORD  C10 " TO Field1
        STORE "LEVEL      C1  " TO Field2
        FOR F = 1 TO 2
          STORE STR(F,1) TO count
          APPEND BLANK
          STORE "Field" + count TO FN
          REPLACE field_name WITH SUBSTR(&FN,1,10)
          REPLACE field_type WITH SUBSTR(&FN,11,1)
          REPLACE field_len  WITH VAL(SUBSTR(&FN,12,2))
          REPLACE field_dec  WITH VAL(SUBSTR(&FN,14,1))
        NEXT
        CREATE PASSWORD FROM DUMMY
        USE PASSWORD
        APPEND BLANK
        REPLACE PASSWORD WITH "SMIS",LEVEL WITH "1"
        INDEX ON PASSWORD TO PASSWORD
        USE
          @15,25 SAY "PASSWORD.DBF is created and indexed"
        ERASE DUMMY.DBF

ENDIF

DO WHILE .T.
   @ 5,0  CLEAR
   SET COLOR TO W+
      @ 3,25 SAY SPACE(30)
      @ 3,33 SAY "PASSWORD ENTRY"
   SET COLOR TO W
   STORE SPACE(10) TO mPW
   STORE SPACE(1)  TO mAL
      @20,31 SAY "Press [F1] for Help."
   SET COLOR TO W+
      @12,28 SAY "Enter your password .... "
   SET COLOR TO W
   SET CONSOLE OFF
   ACCEPT TO mPW
   SET CONSOLE ON
   IF EMPTY(mPW)
      LOOP
   ENDIF
   STORE UPPER(mPW) TO mPW
   USE PASSWORD INDEX PASSWORD
   SET EXACT ON
   FIND "&mPW"
   IF .NOT. FOUND()
      SET EXACT OFF
      USE
      LOOP
```

```
        ELSE
           STORE LEVEL TO mAL
           SET EXACT OFF
           USE
           DO M_MAIN
        ENDIF
    ENDDO
    * End of smis.prg
```

M_MAIN.PRG

```
    * Program ......... m_main
    * Description ...... Main Menu

    DO WHILE .T.
        @ 5,0 CLEAR
       SET COLOR TO W+
          @ 3,25 SAY SPACE(30)
          @ 3,36 SAY "MAIN MENU"
       SET COLOR TO W
       main = 1
       SET MESSAGE TO 22
          @ 8,35 PROMPT "Customers"     MESSAGE SPACE(19)+;
             "Enter, change, or list Customer Information"
          @ 9,35 PROMPT "Orders"        MESSAGE SPACE(19)+;
             "    Enter, change, or list Customer Orders   "
          @10,35 PROMPT "Inventory"     MESSAGE SPACE(19)+;
             "      Enter, change, or list Inventory       "
          @11,35 PROMPT "Salespersons"  MESSAGE SPACE(19)+;
             "      Enter, change, or list Salespersons    "
          @12,35 PROMPT "Passwords"     MESSAGE SPACE(19)+;
             "      Enter, change, or list Passwords       "
          @13,35 PROMPT "Backup"        MESSAGE SPACE(19)+;
             "         Backup or Recall floppy data        "
          @14,35 PROMPT "Return"        MESSAGE SPACE(19)+;
             "          Return to password entry.          "
          @15,35 PROMPT "Quit"          MESSAGE SPACE(19)+;
             "              Quit to DOS.                   "
       MENU TO main
       DO CASE
          CASE main = 1
             DO m_cust
          CASE main = 2
             DO m_ordr
          CASE main = 3
             DO m_inve
          CASE main = 4
             DO m_sale
          CASE main = 5
             DO m_pass
          CASE main = 6
             DO m_data
          CASE main = 7
             @ 5,0 CLEAR
             RETURN
          CASE main = 8
             CLEAR
             QUIT
       ENDCASE
    ENDDO
    RETURN
    * End of m_main.prg
```

M_CUST.PRG

```
* Program .......... m_cust.prg
* Description ...... Customer Menu

DO WHILE .T.
    @ 5,0 CLEAR
   SET COLOR TO W+
    @ 3,25 SAY SPACE(30)
    @ 3,34 SAY "CUSTOMER MENU"
   SET COLOR TO W
   cust = 1
   SET MESSAGE TO 22
    @ 8,37 PROMPT "Enter"    MESSAGE SPACE(28)+;
    "    Enter a new customer.    "
    @ 9,37 PROMPT "Change"   MESSAGE SPACE(28)+;
    "Change or delete a customer."
    @10,37 PROMPT "List"     MESSAGE SPACE(28)+;
    "       List customers.       "
    @11,37 PROMPT "Return"   MESSAGE SPACE(28)+;
    " To return to the Main Menu."
   MENU TO cust
   DO CASE
     CASE cust = 1
       DO e_cust
     CASE cust = 2
       DO c_cust
     CASE cust = 3
       DO l_cust
     CASE cust = 4
       @ 5,0 CLEAR
       RETURN
   ENDCASE
ENDDO
RELEASE ALL
@ 5,0 CLEAR
RETURN
* End of m_cust.prg
```

M_ORDR.PRG

```
* Program .......... m_ordr
* Description ...... Orders Menu

DO WHILE .T.
    @ 5,0  CLEAR
   SET COLOR TO W+
    @ 3,25 SAY SPACE(30)
    @ 3,35 SAY "ORDERS MENU"
   SET COLOR TO W
   ordr1 = 1
   ordr2 = 9
   SET MESSAGE TO 22
    @ 8,37 PROMPT "Enter"    MESSAGE SPACE(28)+;
    "     Enter a new order.      "
    @ 9,37 PROMPT "Change"   MESSAGE SPACE(28)+;
    " Change or delete an order. "
    @10,37 PROMPT "List"     MESSAGE SPACE(28)+;
    "       List sales orders.       "
    @11,37 PROMPT "Return"   MESSAGE SPACE(28)+;
    " To return to the Main Menu."
   MENU TO ordr1
   DO CASE
     CASE ordr1 = 1
       DO e_ordr
     CASE ordr1 = 2
```

```
            DO c_ordr
          CASE ordr1 = 3
            ordr2 = 1
            @10,41 SAY REPLICATE(CHR(196),5)
            @10,46 SAY CHR(191)
            @11,46 SAY CHR(179)
            @12,46 SAY CHR(179)
            @13,42,19,61 BOX mFRAME1
            @13,46 SAY CHR(193)
            @14,43 PROMPT "All Orders        ";
              MESSAGE SPACE(17)+;
              "            To list all orders            "
            @15,43 PROMPT "Customer Select   ";
              MESSAGE SPACE(17)+;
              " To only list orders per a selected customer  "
            @16,43 PROMPT "Item Number Select";
              MESSAGE SPACE(17)+;
              "    To only list orders per a selected item    "
            @17,43 PROMPT "Salesperson Select";
              MESSAGE SPACE(17)+;
              "To only list orders per a selected salesperson"
            @18,43 PROMPT "Return";
              MESSAGE SPACE(17)+;
              "            Return to the Primary Menu"
            MENU TO ordr2
            IF ordr2 = 5
              LOOP
            ELSE
              DO l_ordr WITH ordr2
            ENDIF
          CASE ordr1 = 4
            EXIT
        ENDCASE
    ENDDO
    RELEASE ALL
    @ 5,0 CLEAR
    RETURN
    * End of m_ordr.prg
```

M_INVE.PRG

```
    * Program ......... m_inve.prg
    * Description ...... Inventory Menu

    DO WHILE .T.
        @ 5,0 CLEAR
      SET COLOR TO W+
        @ 3,25 SAY SPACE(30)
        @ 3,33 SAY "INVENTORY MENU"
      SET COLOR TO W
      inve = 1
      SET MESSAGE TO 22
        @ 8,37 PROMPT "Enter"  MESSAGE SPACE(28)+;
          "        Enter a new item.        "
        @ 9,37 PROMPT "Change" MESSAGE SPACE(28)+;
          "   Change or delete an item. "
        @10,37 PROMPT "List"   MESSAGE SPACE(28)+;
          "        List inventory.        "
        @11,37 PROMPT "Return" MESSAGE SPACE(28)+;
          " To return to the Main Menu."
      MENU TO inve
      DO CASE
        CASE inve = 1
          DO e_inve
        CASE inve = 2
          DO c_inve
```

```
              CASE inve = 3
                 DO l_inve
              CASE inve = 4
                 @ 5,0 CLEAR
                 RETURN
           ENDCASE
        ENDDO
        RELEASE ALL
        @ 5,0 CLEAR
        RETURN
        * End of m_inve.prg
```

M_SALE.PRG

```
        * Program .......... m_sale.prg
        * Description ...... Salesperson Menu

        DO WHILE .T.
           @ 5,0 CLEAR
           SET COLOR TO W+
           @ 3,25 SAY SPACE(30)
           @ 3,32 SAY "SALESPERSON MENU"
           SET COLOR TO W
           sale = 1
           SET MESSAGE TO 22
           @ 8,37 PROMPT "Enter"    MESSAGE SPACE(25)+;
              "   Enter a new salesperson.     "
           @ 9,37 PROMPT "Change"   MESSAGE SPACE(25)+;
              "Change or delete a salesperson."
           @10,37 PROMPT "List"     MESSAGE SPACE(25)+;
              "        List salespersons.        "
           @11,37 PROMPT "Return"   MESSAGE SPACE(25)+;
              "  To return to the Main Menu.  "
           MENU TO sale
           DO CASE
              CASE sale = 1
                 DO e_sale
              CASE sale = 2
                 DO c_sale
              CASE sale = 3
                 DO l_sale
              CASE sale = 4
                 @ 5,0 CLEAR
                 RETURN
           ENDCASE
        ENDDO
        RELEASE ALL
        @ 5,0 CLEAR
        RETURN
        * End of m_sale.prg
```

M_PASS.PRG

```
        * Program .......... m_pass.prg
        * Description ...... Password Menu

        DO WHILE .T.
           @ 5,0 CLEAR
           SET COLOR TO W+
           @ 3,25 SAY SPACE(30)
           @ 3,34 SAY "PASSWORD MENU"
           SET COLOR TO W
           pass = 1
           SET MESSAGE TO 22
           @ 8,37 PROMPT "Enter"    MESSAGE SPACE(26)+;
```

```
              "    Enter a new password.      "
           @ 9,37 PROMPT "Change"  MESSAGE SPACE(26)+;
              "Change or delete a password."
           @10,37 PROMPT "List"    MESSAGE SPACE(26)+;
              "      List passwords.          "
           @11,37 PROMPT "Return"  MESSAGE SPACE(26)+;
              " To return to the Main Menu."
        MENU TO pass
        DO CASE
          CASE pass = 1
            DO e_pass
          CASE pass = 2
            DO c_pass
          CASE pass = 3
            DO l_pass
          CASE pass = 4
            @ 5,0 CLEAR
            RETURN
        ENDCASE
     ENDDO
     RELEASE ALL
     @ 5,0 CLEAR
     RETURN
     * End of m_pass.prg
```

M_DATA.PRG

```
     * Program .......... m_data.prg
     * Description ...... Data Backup Menu

     DO WHILE .T.
        @ 5,0 CLEAR
        SET COLOR TO W+
           @ 3,25 SAY SPACE(30)
           @ 3,32 SAY "DATA BACKUP MENU"
        SET COLOR TO W
        data = 1
        SET MESSAGE TO 22
           @ 8,37 PROMPT "Backup"  MESSAGE SPACE(28)+;
              "  Backup data to diskette.  "
           @ 9,37 PROMPT "Change"  MESSAGE SPACE(28)+;
              "     Install backup data.      "
           @10,37 PROMPT "Index"   MESSAGE SPACE(28)+;
              "     Index database files.     "
           @11,37 PROMPT "Return"  MESSAGE SPACE(28)+;
              " To return to the Main Menu."
        MENU TO data
        DO CASE
          CASE data = 1
            DO b_data
          CASE data = 2
            DO r_data
          CASE data = 3
            DO i_data
          CASE data = 4
            @ 5,0 CLEAR
            RETURN
        ENDCASE
     ENDDO
     RELEASE ALL
     @ 5,0 CLEAR
     RETURN
     * End of m_data.prg
```

E__CUST.PRG

```
* Program .......... e_cust.prg
* Description ...... Customer Entry

SET COLOR TO W+
  @ 5,0   CLEAR
  @ 3,25 SAY SPACE(30)
  @ 3,33 SAY "CUSTOMER ENTRY"
SET COLOR TO W
IF ! "&mAL" $ "12"
  DO u_deny
  RETURN
ENDIF
  @ 7,20 SAY "Customer Code ....."
  @ 8,20 SAY "Customer Name ....."
  @ 9,20 SAY "Address ..........."
  @10,20 SAY "City .............."
  @11,20 SAY "State ............."
  @12,20 SAY "Zip Code .........."
  @13,20 SAY "Phone ............."
STORE SPACE(2)  TO mSTATE
STORE SPACE(3)  TO mCUSTCODE
STORE SPACE(5)  TO mZIP
STORE SPACE(12) TO mPHONE
STORE SPACE(20) TO mCUSTNAME,mADDRESS,mCITY
Entering = .T.
DO WHILE Entering
  DO WHILE .T.
    SET COLOR TO W+
      @ 7,20 SAY "Customer Code ....."
    SET COLOR TO W
      @22,26 SAY "Leave blank to return to menu."
      @ 7,40 GET mCUSTCODE PICTURE "@!"
    READ
      @22,0 CLEAR
      @ 7,20 SAY "Customer Code ....."
    IF EMPTY(mCUSTCODE)
      RELEASE ALL
      @ 5,0 CLEAR
      RETURN
    ENDIF
    USE CUST INDEX CUST1
    SEEK mCUSTCODE
    IF FOUND()
      DO u_infi
      STORE SPACE(3) TO mCUSTCODE
      LOOP
    ELSE
      USE
    EXIT
  ENDIF
ENDDO
SET COLOR TO W+
  @ 8,20 SAY "Customer Name ....."
SET COLOR TO W
  @22,26 SAY "Leave blank to return to menu."
  @ 8,40 GET mCUSTNAME
READ
  @22,0 CLEAR
  @ 8,20 SAY "Customer Name ....."
IF EMPTY(mCUSTNAME)
  RELEASE ALL
  @ 5,0 CLEAR
  RETURN
```

```
      ENDIF
      SET COLOR TO W+
         @ 9,20 SAY "Address ..........."
      SET COLOR TO W
         @ 9,40 GET mADDRESS
      READ
         @ 9,20 SAY "Address ..........."
      SET COLOR TO W+
         @10,20 SAY "City .............."
      SET COLOR TO W
         @10,40 GET mCITY
      READ
         @10,20 SAY "City .............."
      SET COLOR TO W+
         @11,20 SAY "State ............."
      SET COLOR TO W
         @11,40 GET mSTATE PICTURE "@!"
      READ
         @11,20 SAY "State ............."
      SET COLOR TO W+
         @12,20 SAY "Zip Code .........."
      SET COLOR TO W
         @12,40 GET mZIP PICTURE "99999"
      READ
         @12,20 SAY "Zip Code .........."
      SET COLOR TO W+
         @13,20 SAY "Phone ............."
      SET COLOR TO W
         @13,40 GET mPHONE PICTURE "999-999-9999"
      READ
         @13,20 SAY "Phone ............."
      Entering = .F.
      DO u_entr
      DO CASE
         CASE mCHOICE = 1
            USE CUST INDEX CUST1
            SET DELETED OFF
            SEEK "???"
            IF FOUND()
               RECALL
            ELSE
               APPEND BLANK
            ENDIF
            REPLACE CUSTCODE WITH mCUSTCODE, CUSTNAME WITH;
               mCUSTNAME, ADDRESS WITH mADDRESS, CITY WITH;
               mCITY, STATE WITH mSTATE, ZIP WITH mZIP
            REPLACE PHONE WITH mPHONE
            SET DELETED ON
            USE
            EXIT
         CASE mCHOICE = 2
            Entering = .T.
            LOOP
         CASE mCHOICE = 3
            EXIT
      ENDCASE
ENDDO Entering
RELEASE ALL
@ 5,0 CLEAR
RETURN
* End of e_cust.prg
```

E__ORDR.PRG

```
* Program .......... e_ordr
* Description ...... Order Entry
```

```
          SET COLOR TO W+
             @ 5,0   CLEAR
             @ 3,25 SAY SPACE(30)
             @ 3,34 SAY "ORDERS ENTRY"
          SET COLOR TO W
          IF ! "&mAL" $ "12"
             DO u_deny
             RETURN
          ENDIF
             @ 7,20 SAY "Order Number ......"
             @ 8,20 SAY "Customer Code ....."
             @ 9,20 SAY "Customer Name ....."
             @10,20 SAY "Salesperson Code .."
             @11,20 SAY "Order Date ........"
             @12,20 SAY "Quantity .........."
             @13,20 SAY "Item Number ......."
             @14,20 SAY "Description ......."
             @15,20 SAY "Unit Cost ........."
             @16,20 SAY "Total Cost ........"
          STORE SPACE(3) TO mORDRNR, mCUSTCODE, mSALECODE, mITEMNR
          STORE DATE()    TO mDATE
          STORE 0         TO mQTY
          USE ORDR INDEX ORDR1
          IF RECCOUNT() = 0
             STORE "  1" TO mORDRNR
          ELSE
             GO BOTTOM
             STORE STR(VAL(ORDRNR)+1,3) TO mORDRNR
          ENDIF
          USE
          SET COLOR TO /W
             @ 7,40 SAY mORDRNR
          SET COLOR TO W
          Entering = .T.
          DO WHILE Entering
             DO WHILE .T.
                SET COLOR TO W+
                   @ 8,20 SAY "Customer Code ....."
                SET COLOR TO W
                   @22,31 SAY "Press [F1] for Help."
                   @24,26 SAY "Leave blank to return to menu."
                   @ 8,40 GET mCUSTCODE PICTURE "@!"
                READ
                   @22,0 CLEAR
                   @ 8,20 SAY "Customer Code ....."
             IF EMPTY(mCUSTCODE)
                RELEASE ALL
                @ 5,0 CLEAR
                RETURN
             ENDIF
             USE CUST INDEX CUST1
             SEEK mCUSTCODE
             IF ! FOUND()
                USE
                DO u_nofi
                STORE SPACE(3) TO mCUSTCODE
                LOOP
             ELSE
                SET COLOR TO /W
                   @ 9,40 SAY CUSTNAME
                SET COLOR TO W
                USE
                EXIT
             ENDIF
          ENDDO
          DO WHILE .T.
```

```
        SET COLOR TO W+
          @10,20 SAY "Salesperson Code .."
        SET COLOR TO W
          @22,31 SAY "Press [F1] for Help."
          @10,40 GET mSALECODE PICTURE "@!"
        READ
          @22,0 CLEAR
          @10,20 SAY "Salesperson Code .."
      IF EMPTY(mSALECODE)
        EXIT
      ENDIF
      USE SALE INDEX SALE1
      SEEK mSALECODE
      IF ! FOUND()
        USE
        DO u_nofi
        STORE SPACE(3) TO mSALECODE
        LOOP
      ELSE
        USE
        EXIT
      ENDIF
    ENDDO
    SET COLOR TO W+
      @11,20 SAY "Order Date ........"
    SET COLOR TO W
      @11,40 GET mDATE PICTURE "99/99/99";
        VALID ! EMPTY(mDATE)
    READ
      @11,20 SAY "Order Date ........"
    SET COLOR TO W+
      @12,20 SAY "Quantity .........."
    SET COLOR TO W
      @12,40 GET mQTY PICTURE "####" VALID ! EMPTY(mQTY)
    READ
      @12,20 SAY "Quantity .........."
    DO WHILE .T.
      SET COLOR TO W+
        @13,20 SAY "Item Number ......."
      SET COLOR TO W
        @22,31 SAY "Press [F1] for Help."
        @13,40 GET mITEMNR PICTURE "###";
          VALID ! EMPTY(mITEMNR)
      READ
        @22,0 CLEAR
        @13,20 SAY "Item Number ......."
      STORE STR(VAL(mITEMNR),3) TO mITEMNR
      SET COLOR TO /W
        @13,40 SAY mITEMNR
      SET COLOR TO W
      USE INVE INDEX INVE1
      SEEK mITEMNR
      IF ! FOUND()
        USE
        DO u_nofi
        STORE SPACE(3) TO mITEMNR
        LOOP
      ELSE
        SET COLOR TO /W
          @14,40 SAY DESC
          @15,40 SAY TRANSFORM(COST,"###,###.##")
          @16,40 SAY TRANSFORM(COST*mQTY,"###,###.##")
        SET COLOR TO W
        USE
        EXIT
      ENDIF
```

```
        ENDDO
        Entering = .F.
        DO u_entr
        DO CASE
          CASE mCHOICE = 1
            USE ORDR INDEX ORDR1
            SET DELETED OFF
            SEEK "???"
            IF FOUND()
              RECALL
            ELSE
              APPEND BLANK
            ENDIF
            REPLACE ORDRNR WITH mORDRNR, CUSTCODE WITH;
              mCUSTCODE, SALECODE WITH mSALECODE, DATE WITH;
              mDATE, QTY WITH mQTY, ITEMNR WITH mITEMNR
            SET DELETED ON
            USE
            EXIT
          CASE mCHOICE = 2
            Entering = .T.
            LOOP
          CASE mCHOICE = 3
            EXIT
        ENDCASE
      ENDDO Entering
      RELEASE ALL
      @ 5,0 CLEAR
      RETURN
      * End of e_ordr.prg
```

E_INVE.PRG

```
    * Program .......... e_inve
    * Description ...... Inventory Entry

SET COLOR TO W+
  @ 5,0  CLEAR
  @ 3,25 SAY SPACE(30)
  @ 3,33 SAY "INVENTORY ENTRY"
SET COLOR TO W
IF ! "&mAL" $ "12"
    DO u_deny
    RETURN
ENDIF
  @ 7,20 SAY "Item Number ......."
  @ 8,20 SAY "Description ......."
  @ 9,20 SAY "Unit Cost ........."
STORE SPACE(3)  TO mITEMNR
STORE SPACE(20) TO mDESC
STORE 0         TO mCOST
USE INVE INDEX INVE1
IF RECCOUNT() = 0
  STORE "  1" TO mITEMNR
ELSE
  GO BOTTOM
  STORE STR(VAL(ITEMNR)+1,3) TO mITEMNR
ENDIF
USE
SET COLOR TO /W
  @ 7,40 SAY mITEMNR
SET COLOR TO W
Entering = .T.
DO WHILE Entering
  SET COLOR TO W+
    @ 8,20 SAY "Description ......."
```

```
    SET COLOR TO W
      @22,26 SAY "Leave blank to return to menu."
      @ 8,40 GET mDESC
    READ
      @22,0 CLEAR
      @ 8,20 SAY "Description ......."
    IF EMPTY(mDESC)
      RELEASE ALL
      @ 5,0 CLEAR
      RETURN
    ENDIF
    SET COLOR TO W+
      @ 9,20 SAY "Unit Cost ........."
    SET COLOR TO W
      @ 9,40 GET mCOST PICTURE "#####.##";
        VALID ! EMPTY(mCOST)
    READ
      @ 9,20 SAY "Unit Cost ........."
    Entering = .F.
    DO u_entr
    DO CASE
      CASE mCHOICE = 1
        USE INVE INDEX INVE1
        SET DELETED OFF
        SEEK "???"
        IF FOUND()
          RECALL
        ELSE
          APPEND BLANK
        ENDIF
        REPLACE ITEMNR WITH mITEMNR, DESC WITH mDESC,;
          COST WITH mCOST
        SET DELETED ON
        USE
        EXIT
      CASE mCHOICE = 2
        Entering = .T.
        LOOP
      CASE mCHOICE = 3
        EXIT
    ENDCASE
  ENDDO Entering
  RELEASE ALL
  @ 5,0 CLEAR
  RETURN
  * End of e_inve.prg
```

E_SALE.PRG

```
  * Program ......... e_sale.prg
  * Description ...... Salesperson Entry

  SET COLOR TO W+
    @ 5,0  CLEAR
    @ 3,25 SAY SPACE(30)
    @ 3,32 SAY "SALESPERSON ENTRY"
  SET COLOR TO W
  IF ! "&mAL" $ "12"
    DO u_deny
    RETURN
  ENDIF
    @ 7,20 SAY "Salesperson Code .."
    @ 8,20 SAY "Salesperson Name .."
    @ 9,20 SAY "Address ..........."
    @10,20 SAY "City .............."
    @11,20 SAY "State ............."
```

```
                     @12,20 SAY "Zip Code .........."
                     @13,20 SAY "Phone ............."
                     @14,20 SAY "Age ..............."
                     @15,20 SAY "Date Hired ........"
                     @16,20 SAY "Base Pay .........."
          STORE SPACE(2)  TO mSTATE
          STORE SPACE(3)  TO mSALECODE
          STORE SPACE(5)  TO mZIP
          STORE SPACE(12) TO mPHONE
          STORE SPACE(20) TO mSALENAME,mADDRESS,mCITY
          STORE DATE()    TO mHIRED
          STORE 0         TO mAGE,mBASEPAY
          Entering = .T.
          DO WHILE Entering
            DO WHILE .T.
              SET COLOR TO W+
                @ 7,20 SAY "Salesperson Code .."
              SET COLOR TO W
                @22,26 SAY "Leave blank to return to menu."
                @ 7,40 GET mSALECODE PICTURE "@!"
              READ
                @22,0 CLEAR
                @ 7,20 SAY "Salesperson Code .."
              IF EMPTY(mSALECODE)
                RELEASE ALL
                @ 5,0 CLEAR
                RETURN
              ENDIF
              USE SALE INDEX SALE1
              SEEK mSALECODE
              IF FOUND()
              DO u_infi
                STORE SPACE(3) TO mSALECODE
              LOOP
            ELSE
              USE
              EXIT
            ENDIF
          ENDDO
          SET COLOR TO W+
            @ 8,20 SAY "Salesperson Name .."
          SET COLOR TO W
            @22,26 SAY "Leave blank to return to menu."
            @ 8,40 GET mSALENAME
          READ
            @22,0 CLEAR
            @ 8,20 SAY "Salesperson Name .."
          IF EMPTY(mSALENAME)
            RELEASE ALL
            @ 5,0 CLEAR
            RETURN
          ENDIF
          SET COLOR TO W+
            @ 9,20 SAY "Address ..........."
          SET COLOR TO W
            @ 9,40 GET mADDRESS
          READ
            @ 9,20 SAY "Address ..........."
          SET COLOR TO W+
            @10,20 SAY "City .............."
          SET COLOR TO W
            @10,40 GET mCITY
          READ
            @10,20 SAY "City .............."
          SET COLOR TO W+
            @11,20 SAY "State ............."
          SET COLOR TO W
```

```
   @11,40 GET mSTATE PICTURE "@!"
READ
   @11,20 SAY "State ............."
SET COLOR TO W+
   @12,20 SAY "Zip Code .........."
SET COLOR TO W
   @12,40 GET mZIP PICTURE "99999"
READ
   @12,20 SAY "Zip Code .........."
SET COLOR TO W+
   @13,20 SAY "Phone ............."
SET COLOR TO W
   @13,40 GET mPHONE PICTURE "999-999-9999"
READ
   @13,20 SAY "Phone ............."
SET COLOR TO W+
   @14,20 SAY "Age ..............."
SET COLOR TO W
   @14,40 GET mAGE PICTURE "##" VALID mAGE > 15
READ
   @14,20 SAY "Age ..............."
SET COLOR TO W+
   @15,20 SAY "Date Hired ........"
SET COLOR TO W
   @15,40 GET mHIRED PICTURE "99/99/99";
     VALID ! EMPTY(mHIRED)
READ
   @15,20 SAY "Date Hired ........"
SET COLOR TO W+
   @16,20 SAY "Base Pay .........."
SET COLOR TO W
   @16,40 GET mBASEPAY PICTURE "###.##";
     VALID ! EMPTY(mBASEPAY)
READ
   @16,20 SAY "Base Pay .........."
Entering = .F.
DO u_entr
DO CASE
   CASE mCHOICE = 1
     USE SALE INDEX SALE1
     SET DELETED OFF
     SEEK "???"
     IF FOUND()
       RECALL
     ELSE
       APPEND BLANK
     ENDIF
     REPLACE SALECODE WITH mSALECODE, SALENAME WITH;
       mSALENAME, ADDRESS WITH mADDRESS, CITY WITH;
       mCITY, STATE WITH mSTATE, ZIP WITH mZIP
     REPLACE PHONE WITH mPHONE, AGE WITH mAGE,;
       HIRED WITH mHIRED, BASEPAY WITH mBASEPAY
     SET DELETED ON
     USE
     EXIT
   CASE mCHOICE = 2
     Entering = .T.
     LOOP
   CASE mCHOICE = 3
     EXIT
   ENDCASE
ENDDO Entering
RELEASE ALL
@ 5,0 CLEAR
RETURN
* End of e_sale.prg
```

E_PASS.PRG

```
* Program .......... e_pass.prg
* Description ...... Password Entry

SET COLOR TO W+
  @ 5,0  CLEAR
  @ 3,25 SAY SPACE(30)
  @ 3,33 SAY "PASSWORD ENTRY"
SET COLOR TO W
IF ! "&mAL" $ "12"
  DO u_deny
  RETURN
ENDIF
  @ 7,25 SAY "Password .........."
  @ 8,25 SAY "Access Level ......"
STORE SPACE(1)  TO mLEVEL
STORE SPACE(10) TO mPASSWORD
Entering = .T.
DO WHILE Entering
  DO WHILE .T.
    SET COLOR TO W+
      @ 7,25 SAY "Password .........."
    SET COLOR TO W
      @22,26 SAY "Leave blank to return to menu."
      @ 7,45 GET mPASSWORD PICTURE "@!"
    READ
      @22,0 CLEAR
      @ 7,25 SAY "Password .........."
    IF EMPTY(mPASSWORD)
      RELEASE ALL
      @ 5,0 CLEAR
      RETURN
    ENDIF
    USE PASSWORD INDEX PASSWORD
    SEEK mPASSWORD
    IF FOUND()
      DO u_infi
      STORE SPACE(10) TO mPASSWORD
      LOOP
    ELSE
      USE
      EXIT
    ENDIF
  ENDDO
  SET COLOR TO W+
    @ 8,25 SAY "Access Level ......"
  SET COLOR TO W
    @22,31 SAY "Press [F1] for Help."
    @24,26 SAY "Leave blank to return to menu."
    @ 8,45 GET mLEVEL PICTURE "9" VALID(mLEVEL $ " 123")
  READ
    @22,0 CLEAR
    @ 8,25 SAY "Access Level ......"
  IF EMPTY(mLEVEL)
    RELEASE ALL
    @ 5,0 CLEAR
    RETURN
  ENDIF
  Entering = .F.
  DO u_entr
  DO CASE
    CASE mCHOICE = 1
      USE PASSWORD INDEX PASSWORD
      SET DELETED OFF
      SEEK "??????????"
```

```
        IF FOUND()
           RECALL
        ELSE
           APPEND BLANK
        ENDIF
        REPLACE PASSWORD WITH mPASSWORD, LEVEL WITH mLEVEL
        SET DELETED ON
        USE
        EXIT
     CASE mCHOICE = 2
        Entering = .T.
        LOOP
     CASE mCHOICE = 3
        EXIT
   ENDCASE
ENDDO Entering
RELEASE ALL
@ 5,0 CLEAR
RETURN
* End of e_pass.prg
```

C__CUST.PRG

```
* Program .......... c_cust.prg
* Description ...... Customer Change/Delete

SET COLOR TO W+
   @ 5,0   CLEAR
   @ 3,25 SAY SPACE(30)
   @ 3,29 SAY "CUSTOMER CHANGE/DELETE"
SET COLOR TO W
IF ! "&mAL" $ "12"
   DO u_deny
   RETURN
ENDIF
   @ 7,20 SAY "Customer Code ....."
   @ 8,20 SAY "Customer Name ....."
   @ 9,20 SAY "Address ..........."
   @10,20 SAY "City .............."
   @11,20 SAY "State ............."
   @12,20 SAY "Zip Code .........."
   @13,20 SAY "Phone ............."
STORE SPACE(3) TO mCUSTCODE
DO WHILE .T.
   SET COLOR TO W+
      @ 7,20 SAY "Customer Code ....."
   SET COLOR TO W
      @22,31 SAY "Press [F1] for Help."
      @24,26 SAY "Leave blank to return to menu."
      @ 7,40 GET mCUSTCODE PICTURE "@!"
   READ
      @22,0 CLEAR
      @ 7,20 SAY "Customer Code ....."
   IF EMPTY(mCUSTCODE)
      RELEASE ALL
      @ 5,0 CLEAR
      RETURN
   ENDIF
   USE CUST INDEX CUST1
   SEEK mCUSTCODE
   IF ! FOUND()
      DO u_nofi
      STORE SPACE(3) TO mCUSTCODE
      LOOP
   ELSE
      STORE CUSTNAME TO mCUSTNAME
```

```
              STORE ADDRESS TO mADDRESS
              STORE CITY TO mCITY
              STORE STATE TO mSTATE
              STORE ZIP TO mZIP
              STORE PHONE TO mPHONE
              USE
              EXIT
          ENDIF
       ENDDO
       SET COLOR TO /W
         @ 8,40 SAY mCUSTNAME
         @ 9,40 SAY mADDRESS
         @10,40 SAY mCITY
         @11,40 SAY mSTATE
         @12,40 SAY mZIP
         @13,40 SAY mPHONE
       SET COLOR TO W
       DO u_chng
       DO CASE
          CASE mCHOICE = 1
             RELEASE ALL
             @ 5,0 CLEAR
             RETURN
          CASE mCHOICE = 3
             DO u_sure
             IF mSURE $ "Yy"
                USE CUST INDEX CUST1
                SEEK mCUSTCODE
                REPLACE CUSTCODE WITH "???"
                DELETE
                USE
             ELSE
                RELEASE ALL
                @ 5,0 CLEAR
                RETURN
             ENDIF
       ENDCASE
       Changing = .T.
       DO WHILE Changing
          SET COLOR TO W+
             @ 8,20 SAY "Customer Name ....."
          SET COLOR TO W
             @ 8,40 GET mCUSTNAME VALID ! EMPTY(mCUSTNAME)
          READ
             @ 8,20 SAY "Customer Name ....."
          SET COLOR TO W+
             @ 9,20 SAY "Address .........."
          SET COLOR TO W
             @ 9,40 GET mADDRESS
          READ
             @ 9,20 SAY "Address .........."
          SET COLOR TO W+
             @10,20 SAY "City ............."
          SET COLOR TO W
             @10,40 GET mCITY
          READ
             @10,20 SAY "City ............."
          SET COLOR TO W+
             @11,20 SAY "State ............"
          SET COLOR TO W
             @11,40 GET mSTATE PICTURE "@!"
          READ
             @11,20 SAY "State ............"
          SET COLOR TO W+
             @12,20 SAY "Zip Code .........."
          SET COLOR TO W
```

```
        @12,40 GET mZIP PICTURE "99999"
     READ
        @12,20 SAY "Zip Code .........."
     SET COLOR TO W+
        @13,20 SAY "Phone ............."
     SET COLOR TO W
        @13,40 GET mPHONE PICTURE "999-999-9999"
     READ
        @13,20 SAY "Phone ............."
     Changing = .F.
     DO u_upda
     DO CASE
        CASE mCHOICE = 1
           USE CUST INDEX CUST1
           SEEK mCUSTCODE
           REPLACE CUSTNAME WITH mCUSTNAME, ADDRESS WITH;
              mADDRESS, CITY WITH mCITY, STATE WITH mSTATE,;
              ZIP WITH mZIP, PHONE WITH mPHONE
           USE
           EXIT
        CASE mCHOICE = 2
           Changing = .T.
           LOOP
        CASE mCHOICE = 3
           EXIT
     ENDCASE
  ENDDO Changing
  RELEASE ALL
  @ 5,0 CLEAR
  RETURN
  * End of c_cust.prg
```

C__ORDR.PRG

```
  * Program .......... c_ordr
  * Description ...... Order Change/Delete

  SET COLOR TO W+
     @ 5,0  CLEAR
     @ 3,25 SAY SPACE(30)
     @ 3,31 SAY "ORDER CHANGE/DELETE"
  SET COLOR TO W
  IF ! "&mAL" $ "12"
     DO u_deny
     RETURN
  ENDIF
     @ 7,20 SAY "Order Number ......"
     @ 8,20 SAY "Customer Code ....."
     @ 9,20 SAY "Customer Name ....."
     @10,20 SAY "Salesperson Code .."
     @11,20 SAY "Order Date ........"
     @12,20 SAY "Quantity .........."
     @13,20 SAY "Item Number ......."
     @14,20 SAY "Description ......."
     @15,20 SAY "Unit Cost ........."
     @16,20 SAY "Total Cost ........"
  STORE SPACE(3) TO mORDRNR
  DO WHILE .T.
     SET COLOR TO W+
        @ 7,20 SAY "Order Number ......"
     SET COLOR TO W
        @22,31 SAY "Press [F1] for Help."
        @24,26 SAY "Leave blank to return to menu."
        @ 7,40 GET mORDRNR PICTURE "###"
     READ
        @22,0 CLEAR
```

```
                         @ 7,20 SAY "Order Number ......"
              IF EMPTY(mORDRNR)
                RELEASE ALL
                @ 5,0 CLEAR
                RETURN
              ENDIF
              STORE STR(VAL(mORDRNR),3) TO mORDRNR
              SET COLOR TO /W
                @ 7,40 SAY mORDRNR
              SET COLOR TO W
              USE ORDR INDEX ORDR1
              SEEK mORDRNR
              IF ! FOUND()
                DO u_nofi
                STORE SPACE(3) TO mORDRNR
                LOOP
                ELSE
                   STORE CUSTCODE TO mCUSTCODE
                   STORE SALECODE TO mSALECODE
                   STORE DATE TO mDATE
                   STORE QTY TO mQTY
                   STORE ITEMNR TO mITEMNR
                   USE
                   EXIT
                ENDIF
              ENDDO
              SET COLOR TO /W
                @ 8,40 SAY mCUSTCODE
                @10,40 SAY mSALECODE
                @11,40 SAY mDATE
                @12,40 SAY STR(mQTY,4)
                @13,40 SAY mITEMNR
              SET COLOR TO W
              USE CUST INDEX CUST1
              SEEK mCUSTCODE
              IF FOUND()
                SET COLOR TO /W
                   @ 9,40 SAY CUSTNAME
                SET COLOR TO W
              ENDIF
              USE INVE INDEX INVE1
              SEEK mITEMNR
              IF FOUND()
                SET COLOR TO /W
                   @14,40 SAY DESC
                   @15,40 SAY TRANSFORM(COST,"###,###.##")
                   @16,40 SAY TRANSFORM(COST*mQTY,"###,###.##")
                SET COLOR TO W
              ENDIF
              USE
              DO u_chng
              DO CASE
                CASE mCHOICE = 1
                   RELEASE ALL
                   @ 5,0 CLEAR
                   RETURN
                CASE mCHOICE = 3
                   DO u_sure
                   IF mSURE $ "Yy"
                     USE ORDR INDEX ORDR1
                     SEEK mORDRNR
                     REPLACE ORDRNR WITH "???"
                     DELETE
                     USE
                   ENDIF
                   RELEASE ALL
```

```
      @ 5,0 CLEAR
      RETURN
ENDCASE
Changing = .T.
DO WHILE Changing
   DO WHILE .T.
      SET COLOR TO W+
         @ 8,20 SAY "Customer Code ....."
      SET COLOR TO W
         @22,31 SAY "Press [F1] for Help."
         @ 8,40 GET mCUSTCODE PICTURE "@!";
            VALID ! EMPTY(mCUSTCODE)
      READ
         @22,0 CLEAR
         @ 8,20 SAY "Customer Code ....."
      USE CUST INDEX CUST1
      SEEK mCUSTCODE
      IF ! FOUND()
         USE
         DO u_nofi
         STORE SPACE(3) TO mCUSTCODE
         LOOP
      ELSE
         SET COLOR TO /W
            @ 9,40 SAY CUSTNAME
         SET COLOR TO W
         USE
         EXIT
      ENDIF
   ENDDO
   DO WHILE .T.
      SET COLOR TO W+
         @10,20 SAY "Salesperson Code .."
      SET COLOR TO W
         @22,31 SAY "Press [F1] for Help."
         @10,40 GET mSALECODE PICTURE "@!"
      READ
         @22,0 CLEAR
         @10,20 SAY "Salesperson Code .."
      IF EMPTY(mSALECODE)
         EXIT
      ENDIF
      USE SALE INDEX SALE1
      SEEK mSALECODE
      IF ! FOUND()
         USE
         DO u_nofi
         STORE SPACE(3) TO mSALECODE
         LOOP
      ELSE
         USE
         EXIT
      ENDIF
   ENDDO
   SET COLOR TO W+
      @11,20 SAY "Order Date ........"
   SET COLOR TO W
      @11,40 GET mDATE PICTURE "99/99/99";
         VALID ! EMPTY(mDATE)
   READ
      @11,20 SAY "Order Date ........"
   SET COLOR TO W+
      @12,20 SAY "Quantity .........."
   SET COLOR TO W
      @12,40 GET mQTY PICTURE "####" VALID ! EMPTY(mQTY)
   READ
```

118

```
                @12,20 SAY "Quantity .........."
            DO WHILE .T.
               SET COLOR TO W+
                 @13,20 SAY "Item Number ......."
               SET COLOR TO W
                 @22,31 SAY "Press [F1] for Help."
                 @13,40 GET mITEMNR PICTURE "###";
                    VALID ! EMPTY(mITEMNR)
               READ
                 @22,0 CLEAR
                 @13,20 SAY "Item Number ......."
               STORE STR(VAL(mITEMNR),3) TO mITEMNR
               SET COLOR TO /W
                 @13,40 SAY mITEMNR
               SET COLOR TO W
               USE INVE INDEX INVE1
               SEEK mITEMNR
               IF ! FOUND()
                 USE
                 DO u_nofi
                 STORE SPACE(3) TO mITEMNR
                 LOOP
               ELSE
                 SET COLOR TO /W
                   @14,40 SAY DESC
                   @15,40 SAY TRANSFORM(COST,"###,###.##")
                   @16,40 SAY TRANSFORM(COST*mQTY,"###,###.##")
                 SET COLOR TO W
                   USE
                   EXIT
                 ENDIF
            ENDDO
            Changing = .F.
            DO u_upda
            DO CASE
               CASE mCHOICE = 1
                 USE ORDR INDEX ORDR1
                 SEEK mORDRNR
                 REPLACE CUSTCODE WITH mCUSTCODE, SALECODE WITH;
                    mSALECODE, DATE WITH mDATE, QTY WITH mQTY,;
                    ITEMNR WITH mITEMNR
                 USE
                 EXIT
               CASE mCHOICE = 2
                 Changing = .T.
                 LOOP
               CASE mCHOICE = 3
                 EXIT
            ENDCASE
         ENDDO Changing
         RELEASE ALL
         @ 5,0 CLEAR
         RETURN
         * End of c_ordr.prg
```

C_INVE.PRG

```
    * Program ......... c_inve
    * Description ...... Inventory Change/Delete

    SET COLOR TO W+
      @ 5,0  CLEAR
      @ 3,25 SAY SPACE(30)
      @ 3,29 SAY "INVENTORY CHANGE/DELETE"
    SET COLOR TO W
    IF ! "&mAL" $ "12"
```

```
      DO u_deny
      RETURN
   ENDIF
      @ 7,20 SAY "Item Number ......."
      @ 8,20 SAY "Description ......."
      @ 9,20 SAY "Unit Cost ........."
   STORE SPACE(3) TO mITEMNR
   DO WHILE .T.
      SET COLOR TO W+
         @ 7,20 SAY "Item Number ......."
      SET COLOR TO W
         @22,31 SAY "Press [F1] for Help."
         @24,26 SAY "Leave blank to return to menu."
         @ 7,40 GET mITEMNR PICTURE "###"
      READ
         @22,0 CLEAR
         @ 7,20 SAY "Item Number ......."
      IF EMPTY(mITEMNR)
         RELEASE ALL
         @ 5,0 CLEAR
         RETURN
      ENDIF
      STORE STR(VAL(mITEMNR),3) TO mITEMNR
      SET COLOR TO /W
         @ 7,40 SAY mITEMNR
      SET COLOR TO W
      USE INVE INDEX INVE1
      SEEK mORDRNR
      IF ! FOUND()
         DO u_nofi
         STORE SPACE(3) TO mITEMNR
         LOOP
      ELSE
         STORE DESC TO mDESC
         STORE COST TO mCOST
         USE
         EXIT
      ENDIF
   ENDDO
   SET COLOR TO /W
      @ 8,40 SAY mDESC
      @ 9,40 SAY TRANSFORM(mCOST,"###,###.##")
   DO u_chng
   DO CASE
      CASE mCHOICE = 1
         RELEASE ALL
         @ 5,0 CLEAR
         RETURN
      CASE mCHOICE = 3
         DO u_sure
         IF mSURE $ "Yy"
            USE INVE INDEX INVE1
            SEEK mORDRNR
            REPLACE ORDRNR WITH "???"
            DELETE
            USE
         ENDIF
         RELEASE ALL
         @ 5,0 CLEAR
         RETURN
   ENDCASE
   Changing = .T.
   DO WHILE Changing
      SET COLOR TO W+
         @ 8,20 SAY "Description ......."
      SET COLOR TO W
```

```
              @ 8,40 GET mDESC VALID ! EMPTY(mDESC)
          READ
              @ 8,20 SAY "Description ......."
          SET COLOR TO W+
              @ 9,20 SAY "Unit Cost ........."
          SET COLOR TO W
              @ 9,40 GET mCOST PICTURE "#####.##";
                 VALID ! EMPTY(mCOST)
          READ
              @ 9,20 SAY "Unit Cost ........."
          Changing = .F.
          DO u_upda
          DO CASE
            CASE mCHOICE = 1
                USE INVE INDEX INVE1
                SEEK mITEMNR
                REPLACE DESC WITH mDESC, COST WITH mCOST
                USE
                EXIT
            CASE mCHOICE = 2
                Changing = .T.
                LOOP
              CASE mCHOICE = 3
                EXIT
            ENDCASE
        ENDDO Changing
        RELEASE ALL
        @ 5,0 CLEAR
        RETURN
        * End of c_inve.prg
```

C_SALE.PRG

```
    * Program .......... c sale.prg
    * Description ...... Salesperson Change/Delete

    SET COLOR TO W+
        @ 5,0  CLEAR
        @ 3,25 SAY SPACE(30)
        @ 3,28 SAY "SALESPERSON CHANGE/DELETE"
    SET COLOR TO W
    IF ! "&mAL" $ "12"
        DO u_deny
        RETURN
    ENDIF
        @ 7,20 SAY "Salesperson Code .."
        @ 8,20 SAY "Salesperson Name .."
        @ 9,20 SAY "Address ..........."
        @10,20 SAY "City .............."
        @11,20 SAY "State ............."
        @12,20 SAY "Zip Code .........."
        @13,20 SAY "Phone ............."
        @14,20 SAY "Age ..............."
        @15,20 SAY "Date Hired ........"
        @16,20 SAY "Base Pay .........."
    STORE SPACE(3) TO mSALECODE
    DO WHILE .T.
        SET COLOR TO W+
            @ 7,20 SAY "Salesperson Code .."
        SET COLOR TO W
            @22,31 SAY "Press [F1] for Help."
            @24,26 SAY "Leave blank to return to menu."
            @ 7,40 GET mSALECODE PICTURE "@!"
        READ
            @22,0 CLEAR
            @ 7,20 SAY "Salesperson Code .."
```

```
    IF EMPTY(mSALECODE)
       RELEASE ALL
       @ 5,0 CLEAR
       RETURN
    ENDIF
    USE SALE INDEX SALE1
    SEEK mSALECODE
    IF ! FOUND()
       DO u_nofi
       STORE SPACE(3) TO mSALECODE
       LOOP
    ELSE
       STORE SALENAME TO mSALENAME
       STORE ADDRESS TO mADDRESS
       STORE CITY TO mCITY
       STORE STATE TO mSTATE
       STORE ZIP TO mZIP
       STORE PHONE TO mPHONE
       STORE AGE TO mAGE
       STORE HIRED TO mHIRED
       STORE BASEPAY TO mBASEPAY
       USE
       EXIT
    ENDIF
ENDDO
SET COLOR TO /W
   @ 8,40 SAY mSALENAME
   @ 9,40 SAY mADDRESS
   @10,40 SAY mCITY
   @11,40 SAY mSTATE
   @12,40 SAY mZIP
   @13,40 SAY mPHONE
   @14,40 SAY STR(mAGE,2)
   @15,40 SAY mHIRED
   @16,40 SAY STR(mBASEPAY,6,2)
SET COLOR TO W
DO u_chng
DO CASE
   CASE mCHOICE = 1
      RELEASE ALL
      @ 5,0 CLEAR
      RETURN
   CASE mCHOICE = 3
      DO u_sure
      IF mSURE $ "Yy"
         USE SALE INDEX SALE1
         SEEK mSALECODE
         REPLACE SALECODE WITH "???"
         DELETE
         USE
      ELSE
         RELEASE ALL
         @ 5,0 CLEAR
         RETURN
      ENDIF
ENDCASE
Changing = .T.
DO WHILE Changing
   SET COLOR TO W+
      @ 8,20 SAY "Salesperson Name .."
   SET COLOR TO W
      @ 8,40 GET mSALENAME VALID ! EMPTY(mSALENAME)
   READ
      @ 8,20 SAY "Salesperson Name .."
   SET COLOR TO W+
      @ 9,20 SAY "Address .........."
```

```
              SET COLOR TO W
                @ 9,40 GET mADDRESS
              READ
                @ 9,20 SAY "Address .........."
              SET COLOR TO W+
                @10,20 SAY "City ............."
              SET COLOR TO W
                @10,40 GET mCITY
              READ
                @10,20 SAY "City ............."
              SET COLOR TO W+
                @11,20 SAY "State ............"
              SET COLOR TO W
                @11,40 GET mSTATE PICTURE "@!"
              READ
                @11,20 SAY "State ............"
              SET COLOR TO W+
                @12,20 SAY "Zip Code .........."
              SET COLOR TO W
                @12,40 GET mZIP PICTURE "99999"
              READ
                @12,20 SAY "Zip Code .........."
              SET COLOR TO W+
                @13,20 SAY "Phone ............"
              SET COLOR TO W
                @13,40 GET mPHONE PICTURE "999-999-9999"
              READ
                @13,20 SAY "Phone ............"
              SET COLOR TO W+
                @14,20 SAY "Age ..............."
              SET COLOR TO W
                @14,40 GET mAGE PICTURE "##" VALID mAGE > 15
              READ
                @14,20 SAY "Age ..............."
              SET COLOR TO W+
                @15,20 SAY "Date Hired ........"
              SET COLOR TO W
                @15,40 GET mHIRED PICTURE "99/99/99";
                   VALID ! EMPTY(mHIRED)
              READ
                @15,20 SAY "Date Hired ........"
              SET COLOR TO W+
                @16,20 SAY "Base Pay .........."
              SET COLOR TO W
                @16,40 GET mBASEPAY PICTURE "###.##";
                   VALID ! EMPTY(mBASEPAY)
              READ
                @16,20 SAY "Base Pay .........."
              Changing = .F.
              DO u_upda
              DO CASE
                CASE mCHOICE = 1
                  USE SALE INDEX SALE1
                  SEEK mSALECODE
                  REPLACE SALENAME WITH mSALENAME, ADDRESS WITH;
                    mADDRESS, CITY WITH mCITY, STATE WITH mSTATE,;
                    ZIP WITH mZIP, PHONE WITH mPHONE, AGE WITH mAGE
                  REPLACE HIRED WITH mHIRED, BASEPAY WITH mBASEPAY
                  USE
                  EXIT
                CASE mCHOICE = 2
                  Changing = .T.
                  LOOP
                CASE mCHOICE = 3
                  EXIT
              ENDCASE
```

```
ENDDO Changing
RELEASE ALL
@ 5,0 CLEAR
RETURN
* End of c_sale.prg
```

C_PASS.PRG

```
* Program ......... c_pass.prg
* Description ...... Password Change/Delete

SET COLOR TO W+
   @ 5,0  CLEAR
   @ 3,25 SAY SPACE(30)
   @ 3,29 SAY "PASSWORD CHANGE/DELETE"
SET COLOR TO W
IF ! "&mAL" $ "1"
   DO u_deny
   RETURN
ENDIF
   @ 7,25 SAY "Password .........."
   @ 8,25 SAY "Access Level ......"
STORE SPACE(10) TO mPASSWORD
DO WHILE .T.
   SET COLOR TO W+
      @ 7,25 SAY "Password .........."
   SET COLOR TO W
      @22,31 SAY "Press [F1] for Help."
      @24,26 SAY "Leave blank to return to menu."
      @ 7,45 GET mPASSWORD PICTURE "@!"
   READ
      @22,0 CLEAR
      @ 7,25 SAY "Password .........."
   IF EMPTY(mPASSWORD)
      RELEASE ALL
      @ 5,0 CLEAR
      RETURN
   ENDIF
   USE PASSWORD INDEX PASSWORD
   SEEK mPASSWORD
   IF ! FOUND()
      DO u_nofi
      STORE SPACE(10) TO mPASSWORD
      LOOP
   ELSE
      STORE LEVEL TO mLEVEL
      USE
      EXIT
   ENDIF
ENDDO
SET COLOR TO /W
   @ 8,45 SAY mLEVEL
SET COLOR TO W
DO u_chng
DO CASE
   CASE mCHOICE = 1
      RELEASE ALL
      @ 5,0 CLEAR
      RETURN
   CASE mCHOICE = 3
      DO u_sure
      IF mSURE $ "Yy"
         USE PASSWORD INDEX PASSWORD
         SEEK mPASSWORD
         REPLACE PASSWORD WITH "??????????"
         DELETE
```

```
            USE
         ELSE
            RELEASE ALL
            @ 5,0 CLEAR
            RETURN
         ENDIF
      ENDCASE
      Changing = .T.
      DO WHILE Changing
         SET COLOR TO W+
            @ 8,25 SAY "Access Level ......"
         SET COLOR TO W
            @22,31 SAY "Press [F1] for Help."
            @ 8,45 GET mLEVEL PICTURE "9" VALID(mLEVEL $ "123")
         READ
            @22,0 CLEAR
            @ 8,25 SAY "Access Level ......"
         Changing = .F.
         DO u_upda
         DO CASE
            CASE mCHOICE = 1
               USE PASSWORD INDEX PASSWORD
               SEEK mPASSWORD
               REPLACE LEVEL WITH mLEVEL
               USE
               EXIT
            CASE mCHOICE = 2
               Changing = .T.
               LOOP
            CASE mCHOICE = 3
               EXIT
         ENDCASE
      ENDDO Changing
      RELEASE ALL
      @ 5,0 CLEAR
      RETURN
      * End of c_pass.prg
```

L__CUST.PRG

```
      * Program .......... l_cust.prg
      * Description ...... Customer List

      SET COLOR TO W+
         @ 5,0  CLEAR
         @ 3,25 SAY SPACE(30)
         @ 3,33 SAY "LIST CUSTOMERS"
      SET COLOR TO W
      IF ! "&mAL" $ "123"
         DO u_deny
         RETURN
      ENDIF
      SET COLOR TO W+
         @ 6,21 SAY "Code    Customer Name          Phone     "
         @ 7,21 SAY "==== ==================== ============"
      SET COLOR TO W
      mCHOICE = 6
      USE CUST INDEX CUST1
      DO WHILE ! EOF()
         @ 8,0
         DISPLAY OFF NEXT 10 SPACE(20)+CUSTCODE+" ",CUSTNAME,;
            PHONE
         IF EOF()
            mCHOICE = 6
         ELSE
```

```
         mCHOICE = 1
      ENDIF
      DO u_list
      DO CASE
         CASE mCHOICE = 1    && Page Forward
            @ 8,0 CLEAR
            IF EOF()
               GO TOP
            ENDIF
            LOOP
         CASE mCHOICE = 2    && Page Backward
            @ 8,0 CLEAR
            SKIP-8
            IF ! BOF()
               SKIP-8
            ENDIF
            LOOP
         CASE mCHOICE = 3    && Go to top of file
            GO TOP
            LOOP
         CASE mCHOICE = 4    && Go to end of file
            GO BOTTOM
            SKIP-8
            LOOP
         CASE mCHOICE = 5    && Print the file
            EXIT
         CASE mCHOICE = 6    && Return to previous menu
            RELEASE ALL
            USE
            @ 5,0 CLEAR
            RETURN
      ENDCASE
   ENDDO
   IF mCHOICE = 5
      IF ! ISPRINTER()
         ? CHR(7)
         SET COLOR TO W+*
            @22,31 SAY "Printer Not Ready!"
         SET COLOR TO W
         ? INKEY(5)
         RELEASE ALL
         @ 5,0 CLEAR
         RETURN
      ENDIF
         @20,0  CLEAR
      SET COLOR TO W+*
         @22,30 SAY 'P r i n t i n g . . .'
      SET COLOR TO W
      SET CONSOLE OFF
      STORE 50 TO mLINE
      STORE  0 TO mPAGE
      SET PRINT ON
      GO TOP
      DO WHILE ! EOF()
         IF mLINE > 40
         IF mPAGE > 0
            ? CHR(12)
         ENDIF
         STORE 1 TO mLINE
         STORE mPAGE+1 TO mPAGE
         ? "      Page No. "+STR(mPAGE,3)
         ? "      ",DATE()
         ?
         ? SPACE(23)+"Sales Management Information System"
         ?
         ?
         ?
```

```
              ? SPACE(36)+"Customers"
              ?
              ?
              ? SPACE(21)+"Code      Customer Name          Phone      "
              ? SPACE(21)+"==== ==================== ============"
            ENDIF
            ? SPACE(21)+CUSTCODE+"  ",CUSTNAME,PHONE
            STORE mLINE+1 TO mLINE
            SKIP
          ENDDO
          ? CHR(12)
          SET PRINT OFF
          SET CONSOLE ON
        ENDIF
        USE
        RELEASE ALL
        @ 5,0 CLEAR
        RETURN
        * End of l_cust.prg
```

L_ORDR.PRG

```
        * Program .......... l_ordr
        * Description ...... Orders List

        PARAMETERS ordr2
        SET COLOR TO W+
          @ 5,0  CLEAR
          @ 3,25 SAY SPACE(30)
          @ 3,35 SAY "LIST ORDERS"
        SET COLOR TO W
        IF ! "&mAL" $ "123"
          DO u_deny
          RETURN
        ENDIF
        DO CASE
          CASE ordr2 = 2
            STORE SPACE(3) TO mCUSTCODE
            DO WHILE .T.
              SET COLOR TO W+
                @ 7,29 SAY "Customer Code ....."
              SET COLOR TO W
                @22,31 SAY "Press [F1] for Help."
                @24,26 SAY "Leave blank to return to menu."
                @ 7,49 GET mCUSTCODE PICTURE "@!"
              READ
                @22,0 CLEAR
                @ 7,29 SAY "Customer Code ....."
              IF EMPTY(mCUSTCODE)
                RELEASE ALL
                @ 5,0 CLEAR
                RETURN
              ENDIF
              USE CUST INDEX CUST1
              SEEK mCUSTCODE
              IF ! FOUND()
                USE
                DO u_nofi
                STORE SPACE(3) TO mCUSTCODE
                LOOP
              ELSE
                USE
                EXIT
              ENDIF
            ENDDO
```

```
CASE ordr2 = 3
   STORE SPACE(3) TO mITEMNR
   DO WHILE .T.
      SET COLOR TO W+
         @ 7,29 SAY "Item Number ......."
      SET COLOR TO W
         @22,31 SAY "Press [F1] for Help."
         @24,26 SAY "Leave blank to return to menu."
         @ 7,49 GET mITEMNR PICTURE "###"
      READ
         @22,0 CLEAR
         @ 7,29 SAY "Item Number ......."
      IF EMPTY(mITEMNR)
         RELEASE ALL
         @ 5,0 CLEAR
         RETURN
      ENDIF
      USE INVE INDEX INVE1
      SEEK mITEMNR
      IF ! FOUND()
         USE
         DO u_nofi
         STORE SPACE(3) TO mITEMNR
         LOOP
      ELSE
         USE
         EXIT
      ENDIF
   ENDDO
CASE ordr2 = 4
   STORE SPACE(3) TO mSALECODE
   DO WHILE .T.
      SET COLOR TO W+
         @ 7,29 SAY "Salesperson Code .."
      SET COLOR TO W
         @22,31 SAY "Press [F1] for Help."
         @24,26 SAY "Leave blank to return to menu."
         @ 7,49 GET mSALECODE PICTURE "@!"
      READ
         @22,0 CLEAR
         @ 7,29 SAY "Salesperson Code .."
      IF EMPTY(mSALECODE)
         RELEASE ALL
         @ 5,0 CLEAR
         RETURN
      ENDIF
      USE SALE INDEX SALE1
      SEEK mSALECODE
      IF ! FOUND()
         USE
         DO u_nofi
         STORE SPACE(3) TO mSALECODE
         LOOP
         ELSE
            USE
            EXIT
         ENDIF
      ENDDO
   OTHERWISE
ENDCASE
SET COLOR TO W+
   @ 6,17 SAY "Order# Cust Sale   Date    Item Quan "+;
   "Total Cost"
   @ 7,17 SAY "====== ==== ==== ======== ==== ==== "+;
   "=========="
SET COLOR TO W
```

```
mCHOICE = 6
USE ORDR INDEX ORDR1
DO CASE
   CASE ordr2 = 2
     COPY TO TEMP FOR CUSTCODE = mCUSTCODE
   CASE ordr2 = 3
     COPY TO TEMP FOR ITEMNR = mITEMNR
   CASE ordr2 = 4
     COPY TO TEMP FOR SALECODE = mSALECODE
   OTHERWISE
ENDCASE
USE
SELECT 2
USE INVE INDEX INVE1
SELECT 1
IF ordr2 = 1
   USE ORDR INDEX ORDR1
ELSE
   USE TEMP
ENDIF
SET RELATION TO ITEMNR INTO B
DO WHILE ! EOF()
   @ 8,0
   DISPLAY OFF NEXT 10 SPACE(18)+ORDRNR+" ",;
     CUSTCODE+" ",SALECODE+" ",DATE,ITEMNR+" ",QTY,;
     TRANSFORM(QTY*B->COST,"###,###.##")
   IF EOF()
     mCHOICE = 6
   ELSE
     mCHOICE = 1
   ENDIF
   DO u_list
   DO CASE
     CASE mCHOICE = 1
       @ 8,0 CLEAR
       IF EOF()
         GO TOP
       ENDIF
       LOOP
     CASE mCHOICE = 2
       @ 8,0 CLEAR
       SKIP-8
       IF ! BOF()
         SKIP-8
       ENDIF
       LOOP
     CASE mCHOICE = 3
       GO TOP
       LOOP
     CASE mCHOICE = 4
       GO BOTTOM
       SKIP-8
       LOOP
     CASE mCHOICE = 5
       EXIT
     CASE mCHOICE = 6
       RELEASE ALL
       USE
       ERASE TEMP.DBF
       @ 5,0 CLEAR
       RETURN
   ENDCASE
ENDDO
IF mCHOICE = 5
   IF ! ISPRINTER()
     ? CHR(7)
```

```
        SET COLOR TO W+*
           @22,31 SAY "Printer Not Ready!"
        SET COLOR TO W
        ? INKEY(5)
        RELEASE ALL
        USE
        ERASE TEMP.DBF
        @ 5,0 CLEAR
        RETURN
     ENDIF
        @20,0  CLEAR
     SET COLOR TO W+*
        @22,30 SAY 'P r i n t i n g . . .'
     SET COLOR TO W
     SET CONSOLE OFF
     STORE 50 TO mLINE
     STORE  0 TO mPAGE
     SET PRINT ON
     GO TOP
     DO WHILE ! EOF()
        IF mLINE > 40
        IF mPAGE > 0
           ? CHR(12)
        ENDIF
        STORE 1 TO mLINE
        STORE mPAGE+1 TO mPAGE
        ? "        Page No. "+STR(mPAGE,3)
        ? "      ",DATE()
        ?
        ? SPACE(23)+"Sales Management Information System"
        ?
        ?
        ?
        ? SPACE(33)+"Customer Orders"
        ?
        ?
        ? SPACE(17)+"Order# Cust Sale   Date    Item Quan "+;
          "Total Cost"
        ? SPACE(17)+"====== ==== ==== ======== ==== ==== "+;
          "=========="
        ENDIF
        ? SPACE(17)+ORDRNR+" ",CUSTCODE+" ",SALECODE+" ",;
          DATE,ITEMNR+" ",QTY,;
          TRANSFORM(QTY*B->COST,"###,###.##")
        STORE mLINE+1 TO mLINE
        SKIP
     ENDDO
     ? CHR(12)
     SET PRINT OFF
     SET CONSOLE ON
  ENDIF
  USE
  ERASE TEMP.DBF
  RELEASE ALL
  @ 5,0 CLEAR
  RETURN
  * End of l_ordr.prg
```

L__INVE.PRG

```
  * Program .......... l_inve.prg
  * Description ...... Inventory List

  SET COLOR TO W+
     @ 5,0  CLEAR
     @ 3,25 SAY SPACE(30)
```

```
      @ 3,33 SAY "LIST INVENTORY"
SET COLOR TO W
IF ! "&mAL" $ "123"
   DO u_deny
   RETURN
ENDIF
SET COLOR TO W+
   @ 6,23 SAY "Item      Description      Unit Cost"
   @ 7,23 SAY "==== ==================== ========="
SET COLOR TO W
mCHOICE = 6
USE INVE INDEX INVE1
DO WHILE ! EOF()
   @ 8,0
   DISPLAY OFF NEXT 10 SPACE(22)+ITEMNR+" ",DESC,;
     TRANSFORM(COST,"##,###.##")
   IF EOF()
     mCHOICE = 6
   ELSE
     mCHOICE = 1
   ENDIF
   DO u_list
   DO CASE
     CASE mCHOICE = 1
       @ 8,0 CLEAR
       IF EOF()
         GO TOP
       ENDIF
       LOOP
     CASE mCHOICE = 2
       @ 8,0 CLEAR
       SKIP-8
       IF ! BOF()
         SKIP-8
       ENDIF
       LOOP
     CASE mCHOICE = 3
       GO TOP
       LOOP
     CASE mCHOICE = 4
       GO BOTTOM
       SKIP-8

       LOOP
     CASE mCHOICE = 5
       EXIT
     CASE mCHOICE = 6
       RELEASE ALL
       USE
       @ 5,0 CLEAR
       RETURN
   ENDCASE
ENDDO
IF mCHOICE = 5
   IF ! ISPRINTER()
     ? CHR(7)
     SET COLOR TO W+*
       @22,31 SAY "Printer Not Ready!"
     SET COLOR TO W
     ? INKEY(5)
     RELEASE ALL
     @ 5,0 CLEAR
     RETURN
   ENDIF
   @20,0  CLEAR
   SET COLOR TO W+*
     @22,30 SAY 'P r i n t i n g  . . .'
```

```
     SET COLOR TO W
     SET CONSOLE OFF
     STORE 50 TO mLINE
     STORE  0 TO mPAGE
     SET PRINT ON
     GO TOP
     DO WHILE ! EOF()
       IF mLINE > 40
       IF mPAGE > 0
         ? CHR(12)
       ENDIF
       STORE 1 TO mLINE
       STORE mPAGE+1 TO mPAGE
       ? "      Page No. "+STR(mPAGE,3)
       ? "      ",DATE()
       ?
       ? SPACE(23)+"Sales Management Information System"
       ?
       ?
       ?
       ? SPACE(36)+"Inventory"
       ?
       ?
       ? SPACE(23)+"Code     Description        Unit Cost"
       ? SPACE(23)+"==== ==================== ========="
       ENDIF
       ? SPACE(23)+ITEMNR+" ",DESC,;
         TRANSFORM(COST,"##,###.##")
       STORE mLINE+1 TO mLINE
       SKIP
     ENDDO
     ? CHR(12)
     SET PRINT OFF
     SET CONSOLE ON
ENDIF
USE
RELEASE ALL
@ 5,0 CLEAR
RETURN
* End of l_inve.prg
```

L__SALE.PRG

```
* Program ......... l_sale.prg
* Description ...... Salesperson List

SET COLOR TO W+
  @ 5,0  CLEAR
  @ 3,25 SAY SPACE(30)
  @ 3,32 SAY "LIST SALESPERSONS"
SET COLOR TO W
IF ! "&mAL" $ "123"
  DO u_deny
  RETURN
ENDIF
SET COLOR TO W+
  @ 6,21 SAY "Code   Salesperson Name      Phone      "
  @ 7,21 SAY "==== ==================== ============"
SET COLOR TO W
mCHOICE = 6
USE SALE INDEX SALE1
DO WHILE ! EOF()
  @ 8,0
  DISPLAY OFF NEXT 10 SPACE(20)+SALECODE+" ",SALENAME,;
    PHONE
```

```
               IF EOF()
                  mCHOICE = 6 ·
               ELSE
                  mCHOICE = 1
               ENDIF
               DO u_list
               DO CASE
                  CASE mCHOICE = 1
                     @ 8,0 CLEAR
                     IF EOF()
                        GO TOP
                     ENDIF
                     LOOP
                  CASE mCHOICE = 2
                     @ 8,0 CLEAR
                     SKIP-8
                     IF ! BOF()
                        SKIP-8
                     ENDIF
                     LOOP
                  CASE mCHOICE = 3
                     GO TOP
                     LOOP
                  CASE mCHOICE = 4
                     GO BOTTOM
                     SKIP-8
                     LOOP
                  CASE mCHOICE = 5
                     EXIT
                  CASE mCHOICE = 6
                     RELEASE ALL
                     USE
                     @ 5,0 CLEAR
                     RETURN
               ENDCASE
            ENDDO
         IF mCHOICE = 5
            IF ! ISPRINTER()
               ? CHR(7)
               SET COLOR TO W+*
                  @22,31 SAY "Printer Not Ready!"
               SET COLOR TO W
               ? INKEY(5)
               RELEASE ALL
               @ 5,0 CLEAR
               RETURN
            ENDIF
               @20,0  CLEAR
            SET COLOR TO W+*
               @22,30 SAY 'P r i n t i n g . . .'
            SET COLOR TO W
            SET CONSOLE OFF
            STORE 50 TO mLINE
            STORE  0 TO mPAGE
            SET PRINT ON
            GO TOP
            DO WHILE ! EOF()
               IF mLINE > 40
               IF mPAGE > 0
                  ? CHR(12)
               ENDIF
               STORE 1 TO mLINE
               STORE mPAGE+1 TO mPAGE
               ? "      Page No. "+STR(mPAGE,3)
               ? "      ",DATE()
               ?
```

```
    ? SPACE(23)+"Sales Management Information System"
    ?
    ?
    ?
    ? SPACE(34)+"Salespersons"
    ?
    ?
    ? SPACE(21)+"Code    Salesperson Name         Phone      "
    ? SPACE(21)+"==== ==================== ============"
    ENDIF
    ? SPACE(21)+SALECODE+" ",SALENAME,PHONE
    STORE mLINE+1 TO mLINE
    SKIP
  ENDDO
  ? CHR(12)
  SET PRINT OFF
  SET CONSOLE ON
ENDIF
USE
RELEASE ALL
@ 5,0 CLEAR
RETURN
* End of l_sale.prg
```

L_PASS.PRG

```
* Program .......... l_pass.prg
* Description ...... Password List

SET COLOR TO W+
  @ 5,0  CLEAR
  @ 3,25 SAY SPACE(30)
  @ 3,33 SAY "LIST PASSWORDS"
SET COLOR TO W
IF ! "&mAL" $ "1"
  DO u_deny
  RETURN
ENDIF
SET COLOR TO W+
  @ 6,32 SAY " Password  Level"
  @ 7,32 SAY "========== ====="
SET COLOR TO W
mCHOICE = 6
USE PASSWORD INDEX PASSWORD
DO WHILE ! EOF()
  @ 8,0
  DISPLAY OFF NEXT 10 SPACE(31)+PASSWORD," "+LEVEL
  IF EOF()
    mCHOICE = 6
  ELSE
    mCHOICE = 1
  ENDIF
  DO u_list
  DO CASE
    CASE mCHOICE = 1
      @ 8,0 CLEAR
      IF EOF()
        GO TOP
      ENDIF
      LOOP
    CASE mCHOICE = 2
      @ 8,0 CLEAR
      SKIP-8
      IF ! BOF()
        SKIP-8
```

134

```
                    ENDIF
                    LOOP
                CASE mCHOICE = 3
                    GO TOP
                    LOOP
                CASE mCHOICE = 4
                    GO BOTTOM
                    SKIP-8
                    LOOP
                CASE mCHOICE = 5
                    EXIT
                CASE mCHOICE = 6
                    RELEASE ALL
                    USE
                    @ 5,0 CLEAR
                    RETURN
            ENDCASE
        ENDDO
        IF mCHOICE = 5
            IF ! ISPRINTER()
                ? CHR(7)
                SET COLOR TO W+*
                    @22,31 SAY "Printer Not Ready!"
                SET COLOR TO W
                ? INKEY(5)
                RELEASE ALL
                @ 5,0 CLEAR
                RETURN
            ENDIF
                @20,0  CLEAR
            SET COLOR TO W+*
                @22,30 SAY 'P r i n t i n g . . .'
            SET COLOR TO W
            SET CONSOLE OFF
            STORE 50 TO mLINE
            STORE  0 TO mPAGE
            SET PRINT ON
            GO TOP
            DO WHILE ! EOF()
                IF mLINE > 40
                IF mPAGE > 0
                    ? CHR(12)
                ENDIF
                STORE 1 TO mLINE
                STORE mPAGE+1 TO mPAGE
                ? "       Page No. "+STR(mPAGE,3)
                ? "       ",DATE()
                ?
                ? SPACE(23)+"Sales Management Information System"
                ?
                ?
                ?
                ? SPACE(36)+"Passwords"
                ?
                ?
                ? SPACE(32)+" Password  Level"
                ? SPACE(32)+"========= ====="
                ENDIF
                ? SPACE(32)+PASSWORD,"  "+LEVEL
                STORE mLINE+1 TO mLINE
                SKIP
            ENDDO
            ? CHR(12)
            SET PRINT OFF
            SET CONSOLE ON
        ENDIF
```

```
    USE
    RELEASE ALL
    @ 5,0 CLEAR
    RETURN
    * End of l_pass.prg
```

B_DATA.PRG

```
    * Program .......... b_data.prg
    * Description ...... Backup to Floppy

    SET COLOR TO W+
       @ 5,0 CLEAR
       @ 3,25 SAY SPACE(30)
       @ 3,35 SAY "DATA BACKUP"
    SET COLOR TO W
       @ 9,20 SAY "Data will be backed up to floppy drive A."
       @11,20 SAY " Insert SMIS backup diskette in drive A. "
       @14,20 SAY "Press any key when ready to continue ...."
    ? INKEY(0)
       @10,0  CLEAR
    drive_let = "A"
    SET COLOR TO W+*
       @22,26 SAY 'P l e a s e    W a i t . . .'
    SET COLOR TO W
    SET CONSOLE OFF
    COPY FILE ORDR.DBF TO A:ORDR.DBF>NUL
    COPY FILE INVE.DBF TO A:INVE.DBF>NUL
    COPY FILE SALE.DBF TO A:SALE.DBF>NUL
    COPY FILE CUST.DBF TO A:CUST.DBF>NUL
    COPY FILE PASSWORD.DBF TO A:PASSWORD.DBF>NUL
    SET CONSOLE ON
    RELEASE ALL
    @ 5,0 CLEAR
    RETURN
    * End of b_data.prg
```

R_DATA.PRG

```
    * Program .......... r_data.prg
    * Description ...... Recall Floppy Data

    SET COLOR TO W+
       @ 5,0 CLEAR
       @ 3,25 SAY SPACE(30)
       @ 3,35 SAY "DATA RECALL"
    SET COLOR TO W
       @ 9,19 SAY "Data will be recalled from floppy drive A."
       @11,19 SAY "  Insert SMIS backup diskette in drive A. "
       @14,19 SAY " Press any key when ready to continue ...."
    ? INKEY(0)
       @10,0  CLEAR
    IF ! FILE("A:ORDR.DBF")
       ? CHR(7)
       SET COLOR TO W+
          @22,23 SAY "Data not found on floppy diskette."
       SET COLOR TO W
          ? INKEY(5)
          @ 5,0 CLEAR
          RETURN
    ENDIF
    SET COLOR TO W+*
       @22,26 SAY 'P l e a s e    W a i t . . .'
    SET COLOR TO W
    COPY FILE A:ORDR.DBF TO ORDR.DBF>NUL
```

136

```
            COPY FILE A:INVE.DBF TO INVE.DBF>NUL
            COPY FILE A:SALE.DBF TO SALE.DBF>NUL
            COPY FILE A:CUST.DBF TO CUST.DBF>NUL
            COPY FILE A:PASSWORD.DBF TO PASSWORD.DBF>NUL
            DO i_data
            SET CONSOLE ON
            @ 5,0 CLEAR
            RETURN
            * End of r_data.prg
```

I_DATA.PRG

```
            * Program .......... i_data.prg
            * Description ...... Database File Index

            SET COLOR TO W+
              @ 5,0  CLEAR
              @ 3,25 SAY SPACE(30)
              @ 3,36 SAY "INDEXING"
            SET COLOR TO W+*
              @22,26 SAY "P l e a s e   W a i t . . ."
            SET COLOR TO W
            USE ORDR
            INDEX ON ORDRNR TO ORDR1
            USE INVE
            INDEX ON ITEMNR TO INVE1
            USE SALE
            INDEX ON SALECODE TO SALE1
            USE CUST
            INDEX ON CUSTCODE TO CUST1
            USE PASSWORD
            INDEX ON PASSWORD TO PASSWORD
            USE
            @ 5,0 CLEAR
            RETURN
            * End of i_data.prg
```

HELP.PRG

```
            * Program .......... help.prg
            * Description ...... Main Help Program

            PARAMETERS prg,line,mvar

            IF prg="HELP" .OR. prg="H_MAIN" .OR. prg="H_CUST" .OR.;
             prg="H_ORDR" .OR. prg="H_INVE" .OR. prg="H_SALE" .OR.;
             prg="H_PASS" .OR. prg="H_DATA"
              RETURN
            ENDIF

            DO CASE
            CASE prg = "SMIS"
              SAVE SCREEN
                @ 5,0 CLEAR
              SET COLOR TO W
                @ 0,70 SAY "<help>"
                @ 8,19,24,61 BOX mFRAME1
                @ 9,21 SAY "Welcome to SMIS ... Sales Management   "
              SET COLOR TO W+
                @ 9,21 SAY "Welcome to SMIS"
              SET COLOR TO W
                @10,21 SAY "Information System. This software will "
                @11,21 SAY "make it easy to track your customers,  "
                @12,21 SAY "orders, and sales. It is based on the  "
                @13,21 SAY "latest database techniques and has been"
                @14,21 SAY "developed by software specialists.     "
```

```
      @15,21 SAY "SMIS is totally menu-driven, meaning  "
      @16,21 SAY "that each activity is accessed by      "
      @17,21 SAY "selection of a menu choice. Menu       "
      @18,21 SAY "choices are scrolled by using the up   "
      @19,21 SAY "arrow, down arrow, left arrow, and     "
      @20,21 SAY "right arrow keys. A selection is made  "
      @21,21 SAY "by pressing the Enter key.             "
      @23,25 SAY "Press any key to continue ... "
? INKEY(15)
      @ 5,0  CLEAR
      @ 8,19,17,61 BOX mFRAME1
      @ 9,21 SAY "Remember, press [F1] if you need more  "
      @10,21 SAY "information about a particular         "
      @11,21 SAY "selection. If this is the first use of "
      @12,21 SAY "SMIS, system passwords have not yet    "
      @13,21 SAY "been assigned. Therefore, at Password  "
      @14,21 SAY "Entry, just type SMIS to get started.  "
      @16,25 SAY "Press any key to continue ... "
? INKEY(15)
RESTORE SCREEN
RETURN
CASE mvar = "MAIN"
   SAVE SCREEN
   @ 5,0 CLEAR
   SET COLOR TO W
      @ 0,70 SAY "<help>"
   DO h_main WITH main
   RESTORE SCREEN
   RETURN
CASE mvar = "CUST"
   SAVE SCREEN
   @ 5,0 CLEAR
   SET COLOR TO W
      @ 0,70 SAY "<help>"
   DO h_cust WITH cust
   RESTORE SCREEN
   RETURN
CASE mvar = "ORDR"
   SAVE SCREEN
   @ 5,0 CLEAR
   SET COLOR TO W
      @ 0,70 SAY "<help>"
   DO h_ordr WITH ordr1, ordr2
   RESTORE SCREEN
   RETURN
CASE mvar = "INVE"
   SAVE SCREEN
   @ 5,0 CLEAR
   SET COLOR TO W
      @ 0,70 SAY "<help>"
   DO h_inve WITH inve
   RESTORE SCREEN
   RETURN
CASE mvar = "SALE"
   SAVE SCREEN
   @ 5,0 CLEAR
   SET COLOR TO W
      @ 0,70 SAY "<help>"
   DO h_sale WITH sale
   RESTORE SCREEN
   RETURN
CASE mvar = "PASS"
   SAVE SCREEN
   @ 5,0 CLEAR
   SET COLOR TO W
      @ 0,70 SAY "<help>"
```

```
            DO h_pass WITH pass
            RESTORE SCREEN
            RETURN
         CASE mvar = "DATA"
            SAVE SCREEN
            @ 5,0 CLEAR
            SET COLOR TO W
               @ 0,70 SAY "<help>"
            DO h_data WITH data
            RESTORE SCREEN
            RETURN
         CASE prg = "U_LIST"
            SAVE SCREEN
               @ 5,0 CLEAR
            SET COLOR TO W
               @ 0,70 SAY "<help>"
            DO CASE
               CASE mCHOICE = 1
                  @ 8,18,15,62 BOX mFRAME1
                  SET COLOR TO W+
                  @ 9,20 SAY "Forward:"
                  SET COLOR TO W
                  @11,20 SAY "To list the next page of"
                  @12,20 SAY "information."
                  @14,20 SAY "Press any key to continue ..."
               CASE mCHOICE = 2
                  @ 8,18,15,62 BOX mFRAME1
                  SET COLOR TO W+
                  @ 9,20 SAY "Backward:"
                  SET COLOR TO W
                  @11,20 SAY "To list the previous page of"
                  @12,20 SAY "information."
                  @14,20 SAY "Press any key to continue ..."
               CASE mCHOICE = 3
                  @ 8,18,14,62 BOX mFRAME1
                  SET COLOR TO W+
                  @ 9,20 SAY "Top:"
                  SET COLOR TO W
                  @11,20 SAY "To list at the top of the file."
                  @13,20 SAY "Press any key to continue ..."
               CASE mCHOICE = 4
                  @ 8,18,14,62 BOX mFRAME1
                  SET COLOR TO W+
                  @ 9,20 SAY "End:"
                  SET COLOR TO W
                  @11,20 SAY "To list at the end of the file."
                  @13,20 SAY "Press any key to continue ..."
               CASE mCHOICE = 5
                  @ 8,18,14,62 BOX mFRAME1
                  SET COLOR TO W+
                  @ 9,20 SAY "Print:"
                  SET COLOR TO W
                  @11,20 SAY "To print the listed information."
                  @13,20 SAY "Press any key to continue ..."
               CASE mCHOICE = 6
                  @ 8,18,14,62 BOX mFRAME1
                  SET COLOR TO W+
                  @ 9,20 SAY "Return:"
                  SET COLOR TO W
                  @11,20 SAY "Returns SMIS to the previous menu."
                  @13,20 SAY "Press any key to continue ..."
            ENDCASE
            ? INKEY(10)
            RESTORE SCREEN
            RETURN
         CASE prg = "U_ENTR"
```

```
SAVE SCREEN
  @ 5,0 CLEAR
SET COLOR TO W
  @ 0,70 SAY "<help>"
DO CASE
  CASE mCHOICE = 1
      @ 8,18,15,62 BOX mFRAME1
    SET COLOR TO W+
      @ 9,20 SAY "Append:"
    SET COLOR TO W
      @11,20 SAY "To append (add) the entered"
      @12,20 SAY "information to the database file."
      @14,20 SAY "Press any key to continue ..."
  CASE mCHOICE = 2
      @ 8,18,15,62 BOX mFRAME1
    SET COLOR TO W+
      @ 9,20 SAY "Change:"
    SET COLOR TO W
      @11,20 SAY "To make changes to the displayed"
      @12,20 SAY "information."
      @14,20 SAY "Press any key to continue ..."
  CASE mCHOICE = 3
      @ 8,18,15,62 BOX mFRAME1
    SET COLOR TO W+
      @ 9,20 SAY "Ignore:"
    SET COLOR TO W
      @11,20 SAY "To ignore this entry and return to"
      @12,20 SAY "the previous menu."
      @14,20 SAY "Press any key to continue ..."
ENDCASE
? INKEY(10)
RESTORE SCREEN
RETURN
  CASE prg = "U_CHNG"
    SAVE SCREEN
      @ 5,0 CLEAR
    SET COLOR TO W
      @ 0,70 SAY "<help>"
    DO CASE
      CASE mCHOICE = 1
          @ 8,18,15,62 BOX mFRAME1
        SET COLOR TO W+
          @ 9,20 SAY "Return:"
        SET COLOR TO W
          @11,20 SAY "To return to the previous menu"
          @12,20 SAY "without making a change or deletion."
          @14,20 SAY "Press any key to continue ..."
      CASE mCHOICE = 2
          @ 8,18,15,62 BOX mFRAME1
        SET COLOR TO W+
          @ 9,20 SAY "Change:"
        SET COLOR TO W
          @11,20 SAY "To make changes to the displayed"
          @12,20 SAY "information."
          @14,20 SAY "Press any key to continue ..."
      CASE mCHOICE = 3
          @ 8,18,15,62 BOX mFRAME1
        SET COLOR TO W+
          @ 9,20 SAY "Delete:"
        SET COLOR TO W
          @11,20 SAY "To delete this entry and return to"
          @12,20 SAY "the previous menu."
          @14,20 SAY "Press any key to continue ..."
    ENDCASE
    ? INKEY(10)
    RESTORE SCREEN
```

```
                RETURN
          CASE prg = "U_UPDA"
             SAVE SCREEN
                @ 5,0 CLEAR
             SET COLOR TO W
                @ 0,70 SAY "<help>"
             DO CASE
                CASE mCHOICE = 1
                     @ 8,18,15,62 BOX mFRAME1
                   SET COLOR TO W+
                     @ 9,20 SAY "Update:"
                   SET COLOR TO W
                     @11,20 SAY "To update the database file with the'
                     @12,20 SAY "displayed information."
                     @14,20 SAY "Press any key to continue ..."
                CASE mCHOICE = 2
                     @ 8,18,15,62 BOX mFRAME1
                   SET COLOR TO W+
                     @ 9,20 SAY "Change:"
                   SET COLOR TO W
                     @11,20 SAY "To make changes to the displayed"
                     @12,20 SAY "information."
                     @14,20 SAY "Press any key to continue ..."
                CASE mCHOICE = 3
                     @ 8,18,15,62 BOX mFRAME1
                   SET COLOR TO W+
                     @ 9,20 SAY "Ignore:"
                   SET COLOR TO W
                     @11,20 SAY "To ignore any changes and return to"
                     @12,20 SAY "the previous menu."
                     @14,20 SAY "Press any key to continue ..."
             ENDCASE
             ? INKEY(10)
             RESTORE SCREEN
             RETURN
          CASE mvar = "MLEVEL"
             SET COLOR TO W
                @ 0,70 SAY "<help>"
                @20,0 CLEAR
                @21,26,24,53 BOX mFRAME1
                @22,28 SAY "1 = Highest Access Level"
                @23,28 SAY "3 = Lowest Access Level"
             ? INKEY(5)
                @20,0  CLEAR
                @ 0,70
             RETURN
          CASE TYPE(mvar) = "D"
             SET COLOR TO W
                @ 0,70 SAY "<help>"
                @20,0 CLEAR
                @21,23,23,57 BOX mFRAME1
                @22,25 SAY "Enter dates in MM/DD/YY format."
             ? INKEY(5)
                @20,0  CLEAR
                @ 0,70
             RETURN
          CASE TYPE(mvar) = "N"
             SET COLOR TO W
                @ 0,70 SAY "<help>"
                @20,0 CLEAR
                @21,27,23,53 BOX mFRAME1
                @22,29 SAY "Enter a numeric amount."
             ? INKEY(5)
                @20,0  CLEAR
                @ 0,70
             RETURN
```

```
CASE mvar = "MSALENAME" .OR. mvar = "MCUSTNAME"
   SET COLOR TO W
      @ 0,70 SAY "<help>"
      @20,0 CLEAR
      @21,31,23,49 BOX mFRAME1
      @22,33 SAY "Enter the name."
   ? INKEY(5)
      @20,0  CLEAR
      @ 0,70
   RETURN
CASE mvar = "MDESC"
   SET COLOR TO W
      @ 0,70 SAY "<help>"
      @20,0 CLEAR
      @21,27,23,52 BOX mFRAME1
      @22,29 SAY "Enter the description."
   ? INKEY(5)
      @20,0  CLEAR
      @ 0,70
   RETURN
CASE mvar = "MADDRESS"
   SET COLOR TO W
      @ 0,70 SAY "<help>"
      @20,0 CLEAR
      @21,21,23,59 BOX mFRAME1
      @22,23 SAY "Enter the street address or PO box."
   ? INKEY(5)
      @20,0  CLEAR
      @ 0,70
   RETURN
CASE mvar = "MCITY"
   SET COLOR TO W
      @ 0,70 SAY "<help>"
      @20,0 CLEAR
      @21,27,23,53 BOX mFRAME1
      @22,29 SAY "Enter the city or town.'
   ? INKEY(5)
      @20,0  CLEAR
      @ 0,70
   RETURN
CASE mvar = "MSTATE"
   SET COLOR TO W
      @ 0,70 SAY "<help>"
      @20,0 CLEAR
      @21,22,23,57 BOX mFRAME1
      @22,24 SAY "Enter the two-letter state code."
   ? INKEY(5)
      @20,0  CLEAR
      @ 0,70
   RETURN
CASE mvar = "MZIP"
   SET COLOR TO W
      @ 0,70 SAY "<help>"
      @20,0 CLEAR
      @21,23,23,56 BOX mFRAME1
      @22,25 SAY "Enter the five-digit zip code."
   ? INKEY(5)
      @20,0  CLEAR
      @ 0,70
   RETURN
CASE mvar = "MPHONE"
   SET COLOR TO W
      @ 0,70 SAY "<help>"
      @20,0 CLEAR
      @21,25,23,55 BOX mFRAME1
      @22,27 SAY "Enter the telephone number."
```

```
       ? INKEY(5)
         @20,0 CLEAR
         @ 0,70
      RETURN
   CASE mvar = "MAGE"
      SET COLOR TO W
         @ 0,70 SAY "<help>"
         @20,0 CLEAR
         @21,25,23,55 BOX mFRAME1
         @22,27 SAY "Enter the saleperson's age."
       ? INKEY(5)
         @20,0 CLEAR
         @ 0,70
      RETURN
   CASE mvar = "MCUSTCODE" .AND. prg != "E_CUST"
      SET COLOR TO W
         @ 0,70 SAY "<help>"
         @20,0 CLEAR
         @20,19,24,61 BOX mFRAME1
         @21,21 SAY "Code      Customer Name      "
         @22,21 SAY "----  --------------------"
         @20,48 SAY CHR(194)
         @21,48 SAY CHR(179)
         @22,48 SAY CHR(195)
         @22,49 SAY REPLICATE(CHR(196),13)
         @22,61 SAY CHR(180)
         @23,48 SAY CHR(179)
         @24,48 SAY CHR(193)
         @21,50 SAY CHR(025)+CHR(024)+"  Select"
         @23,50 SAY CHR(017)+CHR(196)+CHR(217)+ " Enter"
         USE CUST INDEX CUST1
         DO WHILE .T.
           SET COLOR TO W+
             @23,22 SAY CUSTCODE+"  "+CUSTNAME
           SET COLOR TO W
           C=0
           DO WHILE C=0
             C=INKEY()
           ENDDO
           IF C=13
             STORE UPPER(CUSTCODE) TO mCUSTCODE
             EXIT
           ENDIF
           IF C=5
             SKIP -1
             IF BOF()
               GO BOTTOM
             ENDIF
           ENDIF
           IF C=24
             SKIP
             IF EOF()
               GO TOP
             ENDIF
           ENDIF
           IF C=18
             SKIP -10
             IF BOF()
               GO BOTTOM
             ENDIF
           ENDIF
           IF C=3
             SKIP 10
             IF EOF()
               GO TOP
             ENDIF
```

```
    ENDIF
    IF C=1
       GO TOP
    ENDIF
    IF C=6
       GO BOTTOM
    ENDIF
    LOOP
ENDDO
    CLOSE DATABASES
    @20,0 CLEAR
    @ 0,70
    RETURN
CASE mvar = "MSALECODE" .AND. prg != "E_SALE"
    SET COLOR TO W
       @ 0,70 SAY "<help>"
    @20,0 CLEAR
    @20,19,24,61 BOX mFRAME1
    @21,21 SAY "Code     Salesperson Name   "
    @22,21 SAY "----   --------------------"
    @20,48 SAY CHR(194)
    @21,48 SAY CHR(179)
    @22,48 SAY CHR(195)
    @22,49 SAY REPLICATE(CHR(196),13)
    @22,61 SAY CHR(180)
    @23,48 SAY CHR(179)
    @24,48 SAY CHR(193)
    @21,50 SAY CHR(025)+CHR(024)+"  Select"
    @23,50 SAY CHR(017)+CHR(196)+CHR(217)+ " Enter"
    USE SALE INDEX SALE1
    DO WHILE .T.
       SET COLOR TO W+
          @23,22 SAY SALECODE+"   "+SALENAME
       SET COLOR TO W
       C=0
       DO WHILE C=0
          C=INKEY()
       ENDDO
       IF C=13
          STORE UPPER(SALECODE) TO mSALECODE
          EXIT
       ENDIF
       IF C=5
          SKIP -1
          IF BOF()
             GO BOTTOM
          ENDIF
       ENDIF
       IF C=24
          SKIP
          IF EOF()
             GO TOP
          ENDIF
       ENDIF
       IF C=18
          SKIP -10
          IF BOF()
          GO BOTTOM
       ENDIF
    ENDIF
    IF C=3
       SKIP 10
       IF EOF()
          GO TOP
       ENDIF
    ENDIF
```

144

```
                        IF C=1
                          GO TOP
                        ENDIF
                        IF C=6
                          GO BOTTOM
                        ENDIF
                        LOOP
                     ENDDO
                     CLOSE DATABASES
                     @20,0 CLEAR
                     @ 0,70
                     RETURN
                CASE mvar = "MITEMNR" .AND. prg != "E_INVE"
                   SET COLOR TO W
                     @ 0,70 SAY "<help>"
                     @20,0 CLEAR
                     @20,19,24,61 BOX mFRAME1
                     @21,21 SAY "Item        Description      "
                     @22,21 SAY "----   --------------------"
                     @20,48 SAY CHR(194)
                     @21,48 SAY CHR(179)
                     @22,48 SAY CHR(195)
                     @22,49 SAY REPLICATE(CHR(196),13)
                     @22,61 SAY CHR(180)
                     @23,48 SAY CHR(179)
                     @24,48 SAY CHR(193)
                     @21,50 SAY CHR(025)+CHR(024)+"  Select"
                     @23,50 SAY CHR(017)+CHR(196)+CHR(217)+ " Enter"
                     USE INVE INDEX INVE1
                     DO WHILE .T.
                        SET COLOR TO W+
                          @23,22 SAY ITEMNR+"  "+DESC
                        SET COLOR TO W
                        C=0
                        DO WHILE C=0
                          C=INKEY()
                        ENDDO
                        IF C=13
                          STORE ITEMNR TO mITEMNR
                          EXIT
                        ENDIF
                        IF C=5
                          SKIP -1
                          IF BOF()
                            GO BOTTOM
                          ENDIF
                        ENDIF
                        IF C=24
                          SKIP
                          IF EOF()
                            GO TOP
                          ENDIF
                        ENDIF
                        IF C=18
                          SKIP -10
                          IF BOF()
                            GO BOTTOM
                          ENDIF
                        ENDIF
                        IF C=3
                          SKIP 10
                          IF EOF()
                            GO TOP
                          ENDIF
                        ENDIF
                        IF C=1
```

```
                 GO TOP
             ENDIF
             IF C=6
                GO BOTTOM
             ENDIF
          LOOP
       ENDDO
       CLOSE DATABASES
       @20,0 CLEAR
       RETURN
CASE mvar = "MORDRNR" .AND. prg != "E_ORDR"
    SET COLOR TO W
       @ 0,70 SAY "<help>"
       @20,0 CLEAR
       @20,19,24,61 BOX mFRAME1
       @21,21 SAY "Ordr  Cust  Sale    Date  "
       @22,21 SAY "----  ----  ----  --------"
       @20,48 SAY CHR(194)
       @21,48 SAY CHR(179)
       @22,48 SAY CHR(195)
       @22,49 SAY REPLICATE(CHR(196),13)
       @22,61 SAY CHR(180)
       @23,48 SAY CHR(179)
       @24,48 SAY CHR(193)
       @21,50 SAY CHR(025)+CHR(024)+" Select"
       @23,50 SAY CHR(017)+CHR(196)+CHR(217)+ " Enter"
       USE ORDR INDEX ORDR1
       DO WHILE .T.
          SET COLOR TO W+
             @23,22 SAY ORDRNR+" "+CUSTCODE+"    "+SALECODE+;
                "    "+DTOC(DATE)
          SET COLOR TO W
          C=0
          DO WHILE C=0
             C=INKEY()
          ENDDO
          IF C=13
             STORE ORDRNR TO mORDRNR
             EXIT
          ENDIF
          IF C=5
             SKIP -1
             IF BOF()
                GO BOTTOM
             ENDIF
          ENDIF
          IF C=24
             SKIP
             IF EOF()
                GO TOP
             ENDIF
          ENDIF
          IF C=18
             SKIP -10
             IF BOF()
                GO BOTTOM
             ENDIF
          ENDIF
          IF C=3
             SKIP 10
             IF EOF()
                GO TOP
             ENDIF
          ENDIF
          IF C=1
             GO TOP
```

```
                ENDIF
                IF C=6
                  GO BOTTOM
                ENDIF
                LOOP
              ENDDO
              CLOSE DATABASES
              @20,0 CLEAR
              @ 0,70
              RETURN
          CASE mvar = "MPASSWORD" .AND. prg != "E_PASS"
            SET COLOR TO W
              @ 0,70 SAY "<help>"
              @20,0 CLEAR
              @20,19,24,61 BOX mFRAME1
              @21,21 SAY " Password      Access Level "
              @22,21 SAY "----------   --------------"
              @20,48 SAY CHR(194)
              @21,48 SAY CHR(179)
              @22,48 SAY CHR(195)
              @22,49 SAY REPLICATE(CHR(196),13)
              @22,61 SAY CHR(180)
              @23,48 SAY CHR(179)
              @24,48 SAY CHR(193)
              @21,50 SAY CHR(025)+CHR(024)+"  Select"
              @23,50 SAY CHR(017)+CHR(196)+CHR(217)+ " Enter"
              USE PASSWORD INDEX PASSWORD
              DO WHILE .T.
                SET COLOR TO W+
                  @23,21 SAY PASSWORD+SPACE(8)+LEVEL
                SET COLOR TO W
                C=0
                DO WHILE C=0
                  C=INKEY()
                ENDDO
                IF C=13
                  STORE UPPER(PASSWORD) TO mPASSWORD
                  EXIT
                ENDIF
                IF C=5
                  SKIP -1
                  IF BOF()
                    GO BOTTOM
                  ENDIF
                ENDIF
                IF C=24
                  SKIP
                  IF EOF()
                    GO TOP
                  ENDIF
                ENDIF
                IF C=18
                  SKIP -10
                  IF BOF()
                    GO BOTTOM
                  ENDIF
                ENDIF
                IF C=3
                  SKIP 10
                  IF EOF()
                    GO TOP
                  ENDIF
                ENDIF
                IF C=1
                  GO TOP
                ENDIF
```

```
        IF C=6
           GO BOTTOM
        ENDIF
        LOOP
     ENDDO
     CLOSE DATABASES
     @20,0 CLEAR
     @ 0,70
     RETURN
   OTHERWISE
     SAVE SCREEN
     @20,0 CLEAR
     @22,27,24,52 BOX mFRAME1
     @23,29 SAY "Help is not available!"
     ? INKEY(5)
     RESTORE SCREEN
     RETURN
ENDCASE
RETURN
* End of help.prg
```

H__MAIN.PRG

```
* Program .......... h_main.prg
* Description ...... Main Menu Help

PARAMETERS main

DO CASE
   CASE main = 1
      @ 8,18,16,62 BOX mFRAME1
     SET COLOR TO W+
      @ 9,20 SAY "The Customer Menu allows you to:"
     SET COLOR TO W
      @11,20 SAY " 1. Enter a new customer"
      @12,20 SAY " 2. Change or delete a customer"
      @13,20 SAY " 3. List customers"
      @15,20 SAY "Press any key to continue ... "
   CASE main = 2
      @ 8,18,16,62 BOX mFRAME1
     SET COLOR TO W+
      @ 9,20 SAY "The Orders Menu allows you to:"
     SET COLOR TO W
      @11,20 SAY " 1. Enter a new order"
      @12,20 SAY " 2. Change or delete an order"
      @13,20 SAY " 3. List orders"
      @15,20 SAY "Press any key to continue ... "
   CASE main = 3
      @ 8,18,16,62 BOX mFRAME1
     SET COLOR TO W+
      @ 9,20 SAY "The Inventory Menu allows you to:"
     SET COLOR TO W
      @11,20 SAY " 1. Enter a new item"
      @12,20 SAY " 2. Change or delete an item"
      @13,20 SAY " 3. List inventory"
      @15,20 SAY "Press any key to continue ... "
   CASE main = 4
      @ 8,18,16,62 BOX mFRAME1
     SET COLOR TO W+
      @ 9,20 SAY "The Salesperson Menu allows you to:"
     SET COLOR TO W
      @11,20 SAY " 1. Enter a new salesperson"
      @12,20 SAY " 2. Change or delete a salesperson"
      @13,20 SAY " 3. List salespersons"
      @15,20 SAY "Press any key to continue ... "
   CASE main = 5
```

```
                    @ 8,18,16,62 BOX mFRAME1
              SET COLOR TO W+
                    @ 9,20 SAY "The Password Menu allows you to:"
              SET COLOR TO W
                    @11,20 SAY " 1. Enter a new password"
                    @12,20 SAY " 2. Change or delete a password"
                    @13,20 SAY " 3. List passwords"
                    @15,20 SAY "Press any key to continue ... "
           CASE main = 6
                    @ 8,18,16,62 BOX mFRAME1
              SET COLOR TO W+
                    @ 9,20 SAY "The Data Backup Menu allows you to:"
              SET COLOR TO W
                    @11,20 SAY "1. Backup data to diskette"
                    @12,20 SAY "2. Recall data from diskette"
                    @13,20 SAY "3. Index databases"
                    @15,20 SAY "Press any key to continue ... "
           CASE main = 7
                    @ 8,18,15,62 BOX mFRAME1
              SET COLOR TO W+
                    @ 9,20 SAY "Return:"
              SET COLOR TO W
                    @11,20 SAY "Returns SMIS to the password entry"
                    @12,20 SAY "screen."
                    @14,20 SAY "Press any key to continue ... "
           CASE main = 8
                    @ 8,18,14,62 BOX mFRAME1
              SET COLOR TO W+
                    @ 9,20 SAY "Quit:"
              SET COLOR TO W
                    @11,20 SAY "Quit and return to the DOS prompt."
                    @13,20 SAY "Press any key to continue ... "
        ENDCASE
        ? INKEY(10)
        RETURN
        * End of h_main.prg
```

H__CUST.PRG

```
        * Program .......... h_cust.prg
        * Description ...... Customer Menu Help

        PARAMETERS cust

        DO CASE
           CASE cust = 1
                    @ 8,18,22,62 BOX mFRAME1
              SET COLOR TO W+
                    @ 9,20 SAY "Enter:"
              SET COLOR TO W
                    @11,20 SAY "A new customer is added to the customer  "
                    @12,20 SAY "file. Customer information includes:"
                    @13,20 SAY " 1. Customer Code"
                    @14,20 SAY " 2. Customer Name"
                    @15,20 SAY " 3. Address"
                    @16,20 SAY " 4. City"
                    @17,20 SAY " 5. State"
                    @18,20 SAY " 6. Zip"
                    @19,20 SAY " 7. Phone"
                    @21,20 SAY "Press any key to continue ... "
           CASE cust = 2
                    @ 8,18,19,62 BOX mFRAME1
              SET COLOR TO W+
                    @ 9,20 SAY "Change or Delete:"
              SET COLOR TO W
                    @11,20 SAY "Customer information may be changed or"
```

```
            @12,20 SAY "deleted. First, the customer code must"
            @13,20 SAY "be correctly entered. Customer info,"
            @14,20 SAY "except for the customer code, may be"
            @15,20 SAY "changed. If a customer is deleted, it"
            @16,20 SAY "may never be recalled."
            @18,20 SAY "Press any key to continue ... "
      CASE cust = 3
            @ 8,18,17,62 BOX mFRAME1
         SET COLOR TO W+
            @ 9,20 SAY "List:"
         SET COLOR TO W
            @11,20 SAY "Customer information may be listed."
            @12,20 SAY "The customer code, customer name, and"
            @13,20 SAY "phone number are displayed in groups."
            @14,20 SAY "of ten. The listing may be printed."
            @16,20 SAY "Press any key to continue ... "
      CASE cust = 4
            @ 8,18,14,62 BOX mFRAME1
         SET COLOR TO W+
            @ 9,20 SAY "Return:"
         SET COLOR TO W
            @11,20 SAY "Returns SMIS to the Main Menu."
            @13,20 SAY "Press any key to continue ... "
   ENDCASE
   ? INKEY(10)
   RETURN
   * End of h_cust.prg
```

H_ORDR.PRG

```
   * Program ......... h_ordr.prg
   * Description ...... Orders Menu Help

   PARAMETERS ordr1, ordr2

   DO CASE
      CASE ordr1 = 1 .AND. ordr2 = 9
            @ 8,18,21,62 BOX mFRAME1
         SET COLOR TO W+
            @ 9,20 SAY "Enter:"
         SET COLOR TO W
            @11,20 SAY "A new order is added to the customer"
            @12,20 SAY "file. Order information includes:"
            @13,20 SAY " 1. Order Number"
            @14,20 SAY " 2. Customer Code"
            @15,20 SAY " 3. Salesperson Code"
            @16,20 SAY " 4. Quantity"
            @17,20 SAY " 5. Item Number"
            @18,20 SAY " 6. Order Date"
            @20,20 SAY "Press any key to continue ... "
      CASE ordr1 = 2 .AND. ordr2 = 9
            @ 8,18,19,62 BOX mFRAME1
         SET COLOR TO W+
            @ 9,20 SAY "Change or Delete:"
         SET COLOR TO W
            @11,20 SAY "An order may be changed or deleted."
            @12,20 SAY "First, the order number must be"
            @13,20 SAY "entered. Order information, except for"
            @14,20 SAY "the order number, may be changed. If"
            @15,20 SAY "an order is deleted, it may never be"
            @16,20 SAY "recalled."
            @18,20 SAY "Press any key to continue ... "
      CASE ordr1 = 3 .AND. ordr2 = 9
            @ 8,18,19,62 BOX mFRAME1
         SET COLOR TO W+
            @ 9,20 SAY "List:"
```

```
         SET COLOR TO W
            @11,20 SAY "Orders may be listed per selected"
            @12,20 SAY "criteria. Orders may be listed per:"
            @13,20 SAY " 1. All orders"
            @14,20 SAY " 2. Selected Customer Code"
            @15,20 SAY " 3. Selected Item Number"
            @16,20 SAY " 4. Selected Salesperson Code"
            @18,20 SAY "Press any key to continue ... "
      CASE ordr1 = 4 .AND. ordr2 = 9
            @ 8,18,14,62 BOX mFRAME1
         SET COLOR TO W+
            @ 9,20 SAY "Return:"
         SET COLOR TO W
            @11,20 SAY "Returns DEMO to the Main Menu."
            @13,20 SAY "Press any key to continue ... "
      CASE ordr2 = 1
            @ 8,18,15,62 BOX mFRAME1
         SET COLOR TO W+
            @ 9,20 SAY "All Orders:"
         SET COLOR TO W
            @11,20 SAY "All orders will be displayed. The"
            @12,20 SAY "listing may also be printed out."
            @14,20 SAY "Press any key to continue ... "
      CASE ordr2 = 2
            @ 8,18,17,62 BOX mFRAME1
         SET COLOR TO W+
            @ 9,20 SAY "Customer Select:"
         SET COLOR TO W
            @11,20 SAY "You must enter a valid customer code."
            @12,20 SAY "Orders for that customer only will be"
            @13,20 SAY "displayed. The listing may also be"
            @14,20 SAY "printed out."
            @16,20 SAY "Press any key to continue ... "
      CASE ordr2 = 3
            @ 8,18,17,62 BOX mFRAME1
         SET COLOR TO W+
            @ 9,20 SAY "Item Number Select:"
         SET COLOR TO W
            @11,20 SAY "You must enter a valid item number."
            @12,20 SAY "Orders for that item only will be"
            @13,20 SAY "displayed. The listing may also be"
            @14,20 SAY "printed out."
            @16,20 SAY "Press any key to continue ... "
      CASE ordr2 = 4
            @ 8,18,17,62 BOX mFRAME1
         SET COLOR TO W+
            @ 9,20 SAY "Salesperson Select:"
         SET COLOR TO W
            @11,20 SAY "You must enter a valid salesperson."
            @12,20 SAY "Orders for that salesperson only will"
            @13,20 SAY "be displayed. The listing may also be"
            @14,20 SAY "printed out."
            @16,20 SAY "Press any key to continue ... "
      CASE ordr2 = 5
            @ 8,18,14,62 BOX mFRAME1
         SET COLOR TO W+
            @ 9,20 SAY "Return:"
         SET COLOR TO W
            @11,20 SAY "Returns SMIS to the Orders Menu."
            @13,20 SAY "Press any key to continue ... "
ENDCASE
? INKEY(10)
RETURN
* End of h_ordr.prg
```

H_INVE.PRG

```
* Program ......... h_inve.prg
* Description ...... Inventory Menu Help

PARAMETERS inve

DO CASE
   CASE inve = 1
       @ 8,18,19,62 BOX mFRAME1
     SET COLOR TO W+
       @ 9,20 SAY "Enter:"
     SET COLOR TO W
       @11,20 SAY "A new item is added to the inventory"
       @12,20 SAY "file. Inventory information includes:"
       @13,20 SAY " 1. Item Number"
       @14,20 SAY " 2. Description"
       @15,20 SAY " 3. Stock Quantity"
       @16,20 SAY " 4. Unit Cost"
       @18,20 SAY "Press any key to continue ... "
   CASE inve = 2
       @ 8,18,19,62 BOX mFRAME1
     SET COLOR TO W+
       @ 9,20 SAY "Change or Delete:"
     SET COLOR TO W
       @11,20 SAY "Inventory information may be changed"
       @12,20 SAY "or deleted. First, the item number"
       @13,20 SAY "must be entered. Inventory info,"
       @14,20 SAY "except for the item number, may be"
       @15,20 SAY "changed. If an item is deleted, it may"
       @16,20 SAY "never be recalled."
       @18,20 SAY "Press any key to continue ... "
   CASE inve = 3
       @ 8,18,17,62 BOX mFRAME1
     SET COLOR TO W+
       @ 9,20 SAY "List:"
     SET COLOR TO W
       @11,20 SAY "Inventory information may be listed."
       @12,20 SAY "The item number, description, and unit"
       @13,20 SAY "cost are displayed in groups of ten."
       @14,20 SAY "The item information may be printed."
       @16,20 SAY "Press any key to continue ... "
   CASE inve = 4
       @ 8,18,14,62 BOX mFRAME1
     SET COLOR TO W+
       @ 9,20 SAY "Return:"
     SET COLOR TO W
       @11,20 SAY "Returns SMIS to the Main Menu."
       @13,20 SAY "Press any key to continue ... "
ENDCASE
? INKEY(10)
RETURN
* End of h_inve.prg
```

H_SALE.PRG

```
* Program ......... h_sale.prg
* Description ...... Salesperson Menu Help

PARAMETERS sale

DO CASE
   CASE sale = 1
       @ 8,18,21,62 BOX mFRAME1
     SET COLOR TO W+
       @ 9,20 SAY "Enter:"
```

```
                    SET COLOR TO W
                    @11,20 SAY "A new salesperson is added to the"
                    @12,20 SAY "file. Salesperson info includes:"
                    @13,20 SAY " 1. Salesperson Code    7. Phone"
                    @14,20 SAY " 2. Salepsperson Name   8. Age"
                    @15,20 SAY " 3. Address             9. Hired Date"
                    @16,20 SAY " 4. City               10. Base Pay"
                    @17,20 SAY " 5. State"
                    @18,20 SAY " 6. Zip"
                    @20,20 SAY "Press any key to continue ... "
               CASE sale = 2
                    @ 8,18,19,62 BOX mFRAME1
                    SET COLOR TO W+
                    @ 9,20 SAY "Change or Delete:"
                    SET COLOR TO W
                    @11,20 SAY "Salesperson information may be changed"
                    @12,20 SAY "or deleted. First, the salesperson"
                    @13,20 SAY "code must be entered. Salesperson"
                    @14,20 SAY "info, except for the salesperson code,"
                    @15,20 SAY "may be changed. If a salesperson is"
                    @16,20 SAY "it may may never be recalled."
                    @18,20 SAY "Press any key to continue ... "
               CASE sale = 3
                    @ 8,18,17,62 BOX mFRAME1
                    SET COLOR TO W+
                    @ 9,20 SAY "List:"
                    SET COLOR TO W
                    @11,20 SAY "Salesperson information may be listed."
                    @12,20 SAY "The salesperson code, name, and phone"
                    @13,20 SAY "number are displayed in groups of ten."
                    @14,20 SAY "The information may be printed."
          @16,20 SAY "Press any key to continue ... "
               CASE sale = 4
                    @ 8,18,14,62 BOX mFRAME1
                    SET COLOR TO W+
                    @ 9,20 SAY "Return:"
                    SET COLOR TO W
                    @11,20 SAY "Returns SMIS to the Main Menu."
                    @13,20 SAY "Press any key to continue ... "
          ENDCASE
          ? INKEY(10)
          RETURN
          * End of h_sale.prg
```

H_PASS.PRG

```
     * Program .......... h_pass.prg
     * Description ...... Password Menu Help

     PARAMETERS pass

     DO CASE
        CASE pass = 1
             @ 8,18,17,62 BOX mFRAME1
             SET COLOR TO W+
             @ 9,20 SAY "Enter:"
             SET COLOR TO W
             @11,20 SAY "A new password is added to the file."
             @12,20 SAY "Password information includes:"
             @13,20 SAY " 1. Password"
             @14,20 SAY " 2. Access Level"
             @16,20 SAY "Press any key to continue ... "
        CASE pass = 2
             @ 8,18,19,62 BOX mFRAME1
             SET COLOR TO W+
             @ 9,20 SAY "Change or Delete:"
```

```
      SET COLOR TO W
         @11,20 SAY "Password information may be changed or"
         @12,20 SAY "deleted. First, the password code must"
         @13,20 SAY "be correctly entered. The access"
         @14,20 SAY "level, but not the password itself,"
         @15,20 SAY "may be changed. If a password is"
         @16,20 SAY "deleted, it may never be recalled."
         @18,20 SAY "Press any key to continue ... "
      CASE pass = 3
         @ 8,18,17,62 BOX mFRAME1
      SET COLOR TO W+
         @ 9,20 SAY "List:"
      SET COLOR TO W
         @11,20 SAY "Password information may be listed."
         @12,20 SAY "The password and access level are"
         @13,20 SAY "displayed in groups of ten. The"
         @14,20 SAY "information may be printed."
         @16,20 SAY "Press any key to continue ... "
      CASE pass = 4
         @ 8,18,14,62 BOX mFRAME1
      SET COLOR TO W+
         @ 9,20 SAY "Return:"
      SET COLOR TO W
         @11,20 SAY "Returns SMIS to the Main Menu."
         @13,20 SAY "Press any key to continue ... "
   ENDCASE
   ? INKEY(10)
   RETURN
   * End of h_pass.prg
```

H__DATA.PRG

```
   * Program .......... h_data.prg
   * Description ...... Data Backup Menu Help

   PARAMETERS data

   DO CASE
      CASE data = 1
         @ 8,18,17,62 BOX mFRAME1
      SET COLOR TO W+
         @ 9,20 SAY "Backup to diskette:"
      SET COLOR TO W
         @11,20 SAY "Database files are copied from the"
         @12,20 SAY "fixed drive to the floppy drive. A"
         @13,20 SAY "formatted diskette must be placed in"
         @14,20 SAY "floppy drive A: for backup."
         @16,20 SAY "Press any key to continue ... "
      CASE data = 2
         @ 8,18,16,62 BOX mFRAME1
      SET COLOR TO W+
         @ 9,20 SAY "Recall from diskette:"
      SET COLOR TO W
         @11,20 SAY "Backed up data is installed onto the"
         @12,20 SAY "fixed drive. The data backup floppy"
         @13,20 SAY "diskette must be placed in drive A:"
         @15,20 SAY "Press any key to continue ... "
      CASE data = 3
         @ 8,18,14,62 BOX mFRAME1
      SET COLOR TO W+
         @ 9,20 SAY "Index databases:"
      SET COLOR TO W
         @11,20 SAY "The database files are indexed."
         @13,20 SAY "Press any key to continue ... "
      CASE data = 4
         @ 8,18,14,62 BOX mFRAME1
```

154

```
            SET COLOR TO W+
              @ 9,20 SAY "Return:"
            SET COLOR TO W
              @11,20 SAY "Returns SMIS to the Main Menu."
              @13,20 SAY "Press any key to continue ... "
      ENDCASE
      ? INKEY(10)
      RETURN
      * End of h_data.prg
```

U__ENTR.PRG

```
      * Program .......... u_entr.prg
      * Description ...... Entry Utility Menu

      SET COLOR TO W
        @20,0 CLEAR
        @20,18,24,63 BOX mFRAME1
        @22,18 SAY CHR(195)
        @22,19 SAY REPLICATE(CHR(196),44)
        @22,63 SAY CHR(180)
      mCHOICE = 1
      SET MESSAGE TO 23
        @21,23 PROMPT "Append"   MESSAGE SPACE(18)+CHR(179)+;
        "    Append (add) this entry to the file.   "+CHR(179)
        @21,38 PROMPT "Change"   MESSAGE SPACE(18)+CHR(179)+;
        "       Make changes to this entry.       "+CHR(179)
        @21,53 PROMPT "Ignore"   MESSAGE SPACE(18)+CHR(179)+;
        "    Ignore this entry & return to menu.   "+CHR(179)
      MENU TO mCHOICE
      @20,0 CLEAR
      RETURN
      * End of u_entr.prg
```

U__CHNG.PRG

```
      * Program .......... u_chng.prg
      * Description ...... Change Utility Menu

      SET COLOR TO W
        @20,0 CLEAR
        @20,18,24,63 BOX mFRAME1
        @22,18 SAY CHR(195)
        @22,19 SAY REPLICATE(CHR(196),44)
        @22,63 SAY CHR(180)
      mCHOICE = 1
      SET MESSAGE TO 23
        @21,23 PROMPT "Return"   MESSAGE SPACE(18)+CHR(179)+;
        "    Make no changes and return to menu.   "+CHR(179)
        @21,38 PROMPT "Change"   MESSAGE SPACE(18)+CHR(179)+;
        "       Make changes to this entry.       "+CHR(179)
        @21,53 PROMPT "Delete"   MESSAGE SPACE(18)+CHR(179)+;
        "           Delete this entry.           "+CHR(179)
      MENU TO mCHOICE
      @20,0 CLEAR
      RETURN
      * End of u_chng.prg
```

U__UPDA.PRG

```
      * Program .......... u_upda.prg
      * Description ...... Update Utility Menu

      SET COLOR TO W
```

```
        @20,0 CLEAR
        @20,18,24,63 BOX mFRAME1
        @22,18 SAY CHR(195)
        @22,19 SAY REPLICATE(CHR(196),44)
        @22,63 SAY CHR(180)
     mCHOICE = 1
     SET MESSAGE TO 23
        @21,23 PROMPT "Update"   MESSAGE SPACE(18)+CHR(179)+;
        "       Update file with changes made.       "+CHR(179)
        @21,38 PROMPT "Change"   MESSAGE SPACE(18)+CHR(179)+;
        "    Make additional changes to this entry.  "+CHR(179)
        @21,53 PROMPT "Ignore"   MESSAGE SPACE(18)+CHR(179)+;
        "      Ignore changes & return to menu.      "+CHR(179)
     MENU TO mCHOICE
     @20,0 CLEAR
     RETURN
     * End of u_upda.prg
```

U__LIST.PRG

```
     * Program .......... u_list.prg
     * Description ...... List Utility Menu

     SET COLOR TO W
        @20,0 CLEAR
        @20,17,24,62 BOX mFRAME1
        @22,17 SAY CHR(195)
        @22,18 SAY REPLICATE(CHR(196),44)
        @22,62 SAY CHR(180)
     SET MESSAGE TO 23
        @21,19 PROMPT "Forward"  MESSAGE SPACE(17)+CHR(179)+;
        "         Page forward in this file.         "+CHR(179)
        @21,28 PROMPT "Backward" MESSAGE SPACE(17)+CHR(179)+;
        "         Page backward in this file.        "+CHR(179)
        @21,38 PROMPT "Top"      MESSAGE SPACE(17)+CHR(179)+;
        "         Go to the TOP of this file.        "+CHR(179)
        @21,43 PROMPT "End"      MESSAGE SPACE(17)+CHR(179)+;
        "         Go to the END of this file.        "+CHR(179)
        @21,48 PROMPT "Print"    MESSAGE SPACE(17)+CHR(179)+;
        "                Print this file.            "+CHR(179)
        @21,55 PROMPT "Return"   MESSAGE SPACE(17)+CHR(179)+;
        "         Return to the previous menu.       "+CHR(179)
     MENU TO mCHOICE
     @20,0 CLEAR
     RETURN
     * End of u_list.prg
```

U__INFI.PRG

```
     * Program .......... u_infi.prg
     * Description ...... Already in File Utility

     ? CHR(7)
     SET COLOR TO W+*
        @23,32 SAY "Already in file!"
     SET COLOR TO W
     ? INKEY(5)
     @23,0 CLEAR
     RETURN
     * End of u_infi.prg
```

U__NOFI.PRG

```
     * Program .......... u_nofi.prg
     * Description ...... Not Found Utility
```

```
? CHR(7)
SET COLOR TO W+*
  @23,31 SAY "Not Found in files!"
SET COLOR TO W
? INKEY(5)
@23,0 CLEAR
RETURN
* End of u_nofi.prg
```

U_DENY.PRG

```
* Program ......... u_deny.prg
* Description ...... Access Denied Utility

? CHR(7)
SET COLOR TO W+*
  @23,32 SAY "Access is Denied!"
SET COLOR TO W
? INKEY(5)
@23,0 CLEAR
RETURN
* End of u_deny.prg
```

U_SURE.PRG

```
* Program ......... u_sure.prg
* Description ...... Are You Sure Utility

? CHR(7)
SET COLOR TO W+
  @23,31 SAY "Are You Sure (Y/N)?"
DO WHILE .T.
  WAIT "" TO mSURE
  IF mSURE $ "YyNn"
    EXIT
  ELSE
    LOOP
  ENDIF
ENDDO
@23,0 CLEAR
RETURN
* End of u_sure.prg
```

Appendix B

dFILER Utilities

Interactive commands, typically those used at the dot prompt in dBASE, are not a part of Clipper. In normal use, a Clipper-compiled application does not require such commands.

The programmer, however, often needs direct access to a database file. This might be to index or reindex the file, to edit a record, or to append (add) a record. To edit or append a database directly, the programmer would normally have to use dBASE. To index or reindex, the programmer would have to compile a special program, because dBASE and Clipper index files are not compatible.

dFILER was written to serve as a utility that allows the programmer to perform these interactive steps without having to use dBASE or compile a dedicated program. dFILER provides four direct database activities: index, reindex, edit, and append.

Appendix B contains the source code for the dFILER utilities program. Compiling and linking the five program files results in a single executable DFILER.EXE program.

dFILER was created using the original version of Clipper and therefore does not utilize all of the currently available Clipper commands and functions. You might wish to modify the code to accommodate the latest Clipper techniques.

OPERATION

dFILER is accessed by typing DFILER at the DOS prompt. If

dFILER exists on a drive other than the default drive, be sure to specify where dFILER is to be found.

A single main menu will allow you to select any dFILER function. The menu selections are scrolled left or right by the left-arrow or right-arrow keys. As a menu is scrolled, the current option is always highlighted, and a brief description also appears. An option is selected by pressing the Enter key (see Fig. B-1).

An option may also be selected by pressing the key corresponding to the first letter in the option, that is, by pressing I for Index, E for Edit, and so on.

INDEXING

You will first be prompted for the database file name. If the database file exists on a drive other than the default drive, you must specify the drive designator. If the file is not found, an error message will appear before dFILER allows another entry attempt.

You will next be prompted for the index file name. If the index file already exists, dFILER will ask you if you wish to overwrite the existing file.

The database field names (up to the first 42) will be displayed (see Fig. B-2).

You will next be prompted for the index fields. Up to nine index fields may be specified. When you have entered the last index field, just leave a blank and press [ENTER] when the prompt appears.

Fig. B-1. The dFILER main menu screen.

dFILER will display error messages if you enter index fields that are of the logical or memo type.

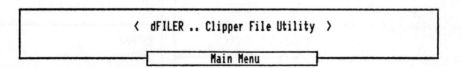

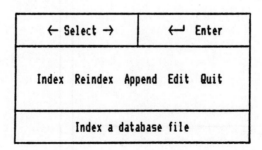

```
< dFILER .. Clipper File Utility >
       INDEX A DATABASE FILE

Database file ..... ORDR              Field Names

Index file ........ ORDR1      ORDRNR
                               CUSTCODE
Index field ....... ORDRNR     SALECODE
Index field .......            QTY
                               ITEMNR
                               DATE
```

Fig. B-2. The dFILER index screen.

```
< dFILER .. Clipper File Utility >
       REINDEX A DATABASE FILE

Database file ..... ORDR              Field Names

Index file ........ ORDR1      ORDRNR
                               CUSTCODE
                               SALECODE
                               QTY
                               ITEMNR
                               DATE



        2 Records Reindexed
```

Fig. B-3. The dFILER Reindex screen.

160

At the conclusion of indexing, the number of indexed records will be displayed; you will then be returned to the main menu.

REINDEXING

Database reindexing follows a very similar procedure as indexing; you will first be prompted for the database file name, then for the index file name. If both of these files are found, the database field names (up to the first 42) will be displayed (see Fig. B-3). Unlike indexing, you are not required to specify index fields at this point. Reindexing takes place automatically.

At the conclusion of reindexing, the number of reindexed records will be displayed; you will then be returned to the main menu.

APPENDING DATA

You will first be prompted for the database file name. If the database file exists on a drive other than the default drive, you must specify the drive designator. If the file is not found, an error message will appear before dFILER allows another entry attempt.

The database field names and blank fields will be displayed and Fig. B-4. The dFILER append you may add data (see Fig. B-4). At the conclusion of adding data, screen. you will be returned to the main menu.

```
              〈  dFILER .. Clipper File Utility  〉

              ┌─────────────────────────────────┐
              ┤      APPEND A DATABASE FILE      ├

    Database file ..... ORDR          Record number .....    2

    ORDRNR      2
    CUSTCODE    JDW
    SALECODE    JAB
    QTY         2
    ITEMNR      1
    DATE        01/02/87
```

```
┌─────────────────────────────────────────────────────────────┐
│           < dFILER .. Clipper File Utility >                │
│          ┌──────────────────────────────────┐                │
│──────────┤        EDIT A DATABASE FILE       ├───────────────│
│          └──────────────────────────────────┘                │
│                                                              │
│  ┌───────────────────────────────────────────────────────┐  │
│  │ Database file ..... ORDR          Record number .....  2 │  │
│  ├───────────────────────────────────────────────────────┤  │
│  │ ORDRNR      2                                          │  │
│  │ CUSTCODE    JDW                                        │  │
│  │ SALECODE    JAB                                        │  │
│  │ QTY         2                                          │  │
│  │ ITEMNR      1                                          │  │
│  │ DATE        01/02/87                                   │  │
│  │                                                        │  │
│  │                                                        │  │
│  │                                                        │  │
│  │                                                        │  │
│  │                                                        │  │
│  │                                                        │  │
│  ├───────────────────────────────────────────────────────┤  │
│  │                                                        │  │
│  └───────────────────────────────────────────────────────┘  │
│                                                              │
└─────────────────────────────────────────────────────────────┘
```

Note that memo fields are displayed as MEMO and may not be appended.

Fig. B-5. The dFILER edit screen.

EDITING DATA

As in the other activities, you will be prompted for the database file name. If the database file exists on a drive other than the default drive, you must specify the drive designator. If the file is not found, an error message will be displayed before dFILER allows another entry attempt.

You will next be prompted for the record number to be edited. If the record number is not found, an error message will be displayed before dFILER allows another entry attempt.

The database field names and blank fields will be displayed and you may edit the data (see Fig. B-5). At the conclusion of editing, you will be prompted to enter another record number; you may leave it blank and press [ENTER] to return to the main menu.

Note that memo fields are displayed as MEMO and may not be edited.

dFILER.PRG

```
* Program Name .......... dFILER.prg
* Description .......... File routines for Clipper

*** Set Environment

set confirm on
set safety off
set scoreboard off
set escape off
set bell off

*** State Public Parameters

public frame1
public frame2
public Delay

*** Define Public Parameters

Delay = 700
frame1 = CHR(218)+CHR(196)+CHR(191)+CHR(179)+;
         CHR(217)+CHR(196)+CHR(192)+CHR(179)
frame2 = CHR(201)+CHR(205)+CHR(187)+CHR(186)+;
         CHR(188)+CHR(205)+CHR(200)+CHR(186)

*** Set up screen

set color to w
clear
  @ 1,0,4,79 BOX frame2
  @ 4,20 say CHR(181)
  @ 4,60 say CHR(198)
set color to w+
  @ 2,19 say '  dFILER .. Clipper Database File Utility

*** Begin Main Menu

do while .T.
  set color to /w
    @ 4,21 say '                    MAIN MENU                   '
  set color to w
    @ 9,20,17,60 BOX frame2
    @ 9,40 say CHR(209)
    @10,40 say CHR(179)
    @11,20 say CHR(199)
    @11,21 say REPLICATE(CHR(196),39)
    @11,60 say CHR(182)
    @11,40 say CHR(193)
    @15,20 say CHR(199)
    @15,21 say REPLICATE(CHR(196),39)
    @15,60 say CHR(182)
    @10,24 say CHR(017)+'- Select -'+CHR(016)
    @10,46 say CHR(017)+CHR(196)+CHR(217)+' Enter'
  H0 = ' Index '
  H1 = ' Reindex '
  H2 = ' Append '
  H3 = ' Edit '
  H4 = ' Quit '
  HLOC=0
  set color to w
    @13,22 say H0
    @13,29 say H1
    @13,38 say H2
    @13,46 say H3
```

```
        @13,52 say H4
do while .T.
  HSET="H"+ltrim(str(HLOC))
  set color to /w
  do case
    case HLOC=0
      @13,22 say H0
      @16,21 say '        Index a database file          '
    case HLOC=1
      @13,29 say H1
      @16,21 say '       Reindex a database file         '
    case HLOC=2
      @13,38 say H2
      @16,21 say '       Append a database file          '
    case HLOC=3
      @13,46 say H3
      @16,21 say '        Edit a database file           '
    case HLOC=4
      @13,52 say H4
      @16,21 say '            Quit to DOS                '
  endcase
  set color to w
    @ 4,79 say ''
  Key=0
  do while Key=0
    Key=inkey()
  enddo
  do case
    case HLOC=0
      @13,22 say H0
    case HLOC=1
      @13,29 say H1
    case HLOC=2
      @13,38 say H2
    case HLOC=3
      @13,46 say H3
    case HLOC=4
      @13,52 say H4
  endcase
  if chr(Key) $ "IiRrAaEeQq"
    if chr(Key) $ "Ii"
      HLOC=0
      exit
    endif
    if chr(Key) $ "Rr"
      HLOC=1
      exit
    endif
    if chr(Key) $ "Aa"
      HLOC=2
      exit
    endif
    if chr(Key) $ "Ee"
      HLOC=3
      exit
    endif
    if chr(Key) $ "Qq"
      HLOC=4
      exit
    endif
  endif
  if Key=13        && Enter key
    exit
  endif
  if Key=19        && Left-cursor key
    HLOC=HLOC-1
```

```
      if HLOC<0
        HLOC=4
      endif
      loop
    endif
    if Key=4          && Right-cursor key
      HLOC=HLOC+1
      if HLOC>4
        HLOC=0
      endif
      loop
    endif
    if Key=1          && Home key
      HLOC=0
          loop
        endif
        if Key=6          && End key
          HLOC=4
          loop
        endif
      enddo
      @ 5,0 clear
      do case
        case HLOC=0
          do dINDEX
        case HLOC=1
          do dREINDEX
        case HLOC=2
          do dAPPEND
        case HLOC=3
          do dEDIT
        case HLOC=4
          clear
          quit
      endcase
    enddo
    return
```

dINDEX.PRG

```
* Program Name .......... dINDEX.prg
* Description ........... Index routine for Clipper

*** Set up screen

set color to /w
  @ 4,21 say '            INDEX A DATABASE FILE
set color to w
  @ 6,0,24,36 box frame2
  @ 8,0  say chr(199)
  @ 8,36 say chr(182)
  @ 8,1  say replicate(chr(196),35)
  @10,0  say chr(199)
  @10,36 say chr(182)
  @10,1  say replicate(chr(196),35)
  @22,0  say chr(199)
  @22,36 say chr(182)
  @22,1  say replicate(chr(196),35)
  @ 7,2  say 'Database file .....'
  @ 9,2  say 'Index file ........'

*** Set memvars

store space(10) to mFNAME
store space(10) to mINAME
store space(10) to mIFIELD
```

```
store space(1)  to mIFORMULA

*** Enter database file name

do while .T.
   set color to w+
     @ 7,2  say 'Database file .....'
     @23,4  say '[ENTER] = return to Main Menu'
   set color to w
     @ 7,22 get mFNAME picture '@!'
   read
     @23,4  say space(29)
   if mFNAME = space(10)
     @ 5,0 clear
     return
   endif
   store mFNAME+".DBF" to mDBFNAME
   if file('&mDBFNAME')
     exit
   else
     ? chr(7)
     set color to w+*

       @23,13 say 'Not Found!'
     set color to w
       @ 4,79 say ''
     X=0
     do while X < Delay
       X=X+1
     enddo
       @23,13 say space(10)
     store space(10) to mFNAME
     loop
   endif
enddo
  @ 7,2  say 'Database file .....'
use &mFNAME

*** Enter index file name

do while .T.
   set color to w+
     @ 9,2  say 'Index file ........'
     @23,4  say '[ENTER] = return to Main Menu'
   set color to w
     @ 9,22 get mINAME picture '@!'
   read
     @23,4  say space(29)
   if mINAME = space(10)
     close databases
     @ 5,0 clear
     return
   endif
   store mINAME+".NTX" to mNTXNAME
   if .not. file('&mNTXNAME')
     exit
   else
     ? chr(7)
     do while .t.
       set color to w+
         @23,2  say 'Already exists. Overwrite? (y/n)'
       set color to w
         @ 4,79 say ''
       set console off
       wait '' to overwrite
       set console on
       if overwrite $ "NnYy"
```

```
        exit
      else
        loop
      endif
      enddo
        @23,2  say space(32)
      if overwrite $ "Nn"
        store space(10) to mINAME
        loop
      else
        exit
      endif
    endif
  endif
enddo
  @ 9,2  say 'Index file ........'

*** Display database fields

set color to w
  @ 6,39,24,79 box frame2
  @ 8,39 say chr(199)
  @ 8,79 say chr(182)
  @ 8,40 say replicate(chr(196),39)
set color to w+
  @ 7,54 say 'Field Names'
set color to w
m=1
row = 9
column = 41
do while m < 43
  for j=m to m+14
    @ row,column say fieldname(j)
  row=row+1
  next
  if "" = fieldname(j)
    exit
  else
    row=9
    m=m+14
    column=column+13
  endif
enddo

*** Enter index fields

i=0
do while .T.
  if i>9
    exit
  endif
  set color to w+
    @11+i,2  say 'Index field .......'
if i=0
  @23,4  say '[ENTER] = return to Main Menu'
endif
set color to w
  @11+i,22 get mIFIELD picture '@!'
read
  @23,4  say space(32)
clear gets
if mIFIELD = space(10)
  if i=0
    close databases
    @ 5,0 clear
    return
  else
    exit
```

```
      endif
    endif
    if type("&mIFIELD")="U"
      ? chr(7)
      set color to w+*
        @23,7 say 'Not a good field name!'
      set color to w
        @ 4,79 say ''
      x = 0
      do while x < Delay
        x = x + 1
      enddo
        @23,7 say space(22)
      store space(10) to mIFIELD
      loop
    endif
    if type("&mIFIELD")="M"
      ? chr(7)
      set color to w+*
        @23,5 say "Can't index a memo field!"
      set color to w
        @ 4,79 say ''
      x = 0
      do while x < Delay
        x = x + 1
      enddo
        @23,5 say space(25)
      store space(10) to mIFIELD
      loop
    endif
    if type("&mIFIELD")="L"
      ? chr(7)
      set color to w+*

        @23,5 say "Can't index a logic field!"
      set color to w
        @ 4,79 say ''
      x = 0
      do while x < Delay
        x = x + 1
      enddo
        @23,5 say space(26)
      store space(10) to mIFIELD
      loop
    endif
    if type("&mIFIELD")="N"
      mIFIELD="STR(&mIFIELD)"
    endif
    if type("&mIFIELD")="D"
      mIFIELD="DTOC(&mIFIELD)"
    endif
    store trim(mIFIELD) to mIFLD
    store space(10) to mIFIELD
    if i=0
      store mIFORMULA + mIFLD to mIFORMULA
    else
      store mIFORMULA + '+' + mIFLD to mIFORMULA
    endif
      @11+i,2  say 'Index field .......'
    i=i+1
    loop
  enddo
  @11+i,2  say space(32)
  @ 4,79 say ''

*** Index the database
```

```
      INDEX ON &mIFORMULA to &mINAME

      *** Display index total

      store ltrim(str(reccount())) to mTOTAL
      set color to w+
        @23,12-len(mTOTAL) say mTOTAL + " Records Indexed"
      set color to w
        @ 4,79 say ''
      x=0
      do while x < 2*Delay
        x = x + 1
      enddo
      close databases
        @ 5,0 clear
      return
```

dREINDEX.PRG

```
      * Program Name ......... dREINDEX.prg
      * Description .......... Reindex routine for Clipper

      *** Set up screen

      set color to /w
        @ 4,21 say '            REINDEX A DATABASE FILE            '
      set color to w
        @ 6,0,24,36 box frame2
        @ 8,0   say chr(199)
        @ 8,36  say chr(182)
        @ 8,1   say replicate(chr(196),35)
        @10,0   say chr(199)
        @10,36  say chr(182)
        @10,1   say replicate(chr(196),35)
        @22,0   say chr(199)
        @22,36  say chr(182)
        @22,1   say replicate(chr(196),35)
        @ 7,2   say 'Database file .....'
        @ 9,2   say 'Index file ........'

      *** Set memvars

      store space(10) to mFNAME
      store space(10) to mINAME

      *** Enter database file name

      do while .T.
        set color to w+
          @ 7,2  say 'Database file .....'
          @23,4  say '[ENTER] = return to Main Menu'
        set color to w
          @ 7,22 get mFNAME picture '@!'
        read
          @23,4  say space(29)
        if mFNAME = space(10)
          @ 5,0 clear
          return
        endif
        store mFNAME+".DBF" to mDBFNAME
        if file('&mDBFNAME')
          exit
        else
          ? CHR(7)
          set color to w+*
            @23,13 say 'Not Found!'
```

```
        set color to w
          @ 4,79 say ''
        x=0
        do while x < Delay
          x = x + 1
        enddo
          @23,13 say SPACE(10)
        store space(10) to mFNAME
        loop
      endif
    enddo
      @ 7,2  say 'Database file .....'

*** Enter index file name

    do while .T.
      set color to w+
        @ 9,2  say 'Index file ........'
        @23,4  say '[ENTER] = return to Main Menu'
      set color to w
        @ 9,22 get mINAME picture '@!'
      read
        @23,4  say space(29)
      if mINAME = space(10)
        @ 5,0 clear
        return
      endif
      store mINAME+".NTX" to mNTXNAME
      if file('&mNTXNAME')
        exit
      else
        ? CHR(7)
        set color to w+*
          @23,13 say 'Not Found!'
        set color to w
          @ 4,79 say ''
        X=0
        do while X < Delay
          X=X+1
        enddo
          @23,13 say space(10)
        store space(10) to mINAME
        loop
      endif
    enddo
      @ 9,2  say 'Index file ........'

*** Display database fields

    use &mFNAME index &mINAME
    set color to w
      @ 6,39,24,79 box frame2
      @ 8,39 say chr(199)
      @ 8,79 say chr(182)
      @ 8,40 say replicate(chr(196),39)
    set color to w+
      @ 7,54 say 'Field Names'
    set color to w
    m=1
    row = 9
    column = 41
    do while m < 43
      for j=m to m+14
        @ row,column say fieldname(j)
        row=row+1
      next
```

```
      if "" = fieldname(j)
        exit
      else
        row=9
        m=m+14
        column = column + 13
        j=j+1
      endif
  enddo
    @ 4,79 say ''

*** Reindex the database

REINDEX

*** Display index total

store ltrim(str(reccount())) to mTOTAL
set color to w+
    @23,11-len(mTOTAL) say mTOTAL + " Records Reindexed"
set color to w
    @ 4,79 say ''
x=0
do while x < 2*Delay
  x = x + 1
enddo
close databases
    @ 5,0 clear
return
```

dEDIT.PRG

```
* Program Name .......... dEDIT.prg
* Description ........... Edit routine for Clipper

*** Set up screen

set color to /w
    @ 4,21 say '              EDIT A DATABASE FILE
set color to w
    @ 6,0,8,79 box frame2
    @22,0,24,79 box frame2
    @ 8,0  say chr(211)
    @ 8,1 say replicate(chr(196),78)
    @ 8,79 say chr(189)
    @22,0  say chr(214)
    @22,1 say replicate(chr(196),78)
    @22,79 say chr(183)
    @ 7,2  say 'Database file .....'
    @ 7,42 say 'Record number .....'

*** Set memvars

store space(10) to mFILENAME
store space(14) to mDBFNAME

*** Enter file name

do while .T.
  set color to w+
    @ 7,2  say 'Database file .....'
    @23,26 say '[ENTER] = return to Main Menu'
  set color to w
    @ 7,22 get mFILENAME picture '@!'
  read
    @23,26 say space(29)
```

```
   if mFILENAME = space(10)
     @ 5,0 clear
     return
   endif
   store mFILENAME+".DBF" to mDBFNAME
   if file('&mDBFNAME')
     exit
   else
     ? chr(7)
     set color to w+*
       @23,35 say 'Not Found!'
     set color to w
       @ 4,79 say ''
     X=0
     do while X < Delay
       X=X+1
     enddo
       @23,35 say space(10)
     store space(10) to mFILENAME
     loop
   endif
enddo
   @ 7,2  say 'Database file .....'

*** Enter record number

do while .T.
   store 0 to mRECNR
   do while .T.
     set color to w+
       @ 7,42 say 'Record number .....'
       @23,26 say '[ENTER] = return to Main Menu'
     set color to w
       @ 7,62 get mRECNR picture '######'
     read
       @23,26 say space(29)
     if mRECNR = 0
       @ 5,0 clear
       return
     endif
     set color to /w
       @ 7,62 say str(mRECNR,6)
     set color to w
     use &mFILENAME
     go bottom
     if mRECNR <= RECNO()
       exit
     else
       ? CHR(7)
       set color to w+*
         @23,35 say 'Not Found!'
       set color to w
         @ 4,79 say ''
       x=0
       do while x < Delay
         x = x + 1
       enddo
         @23,35 say space(10)
       store 0 to mRECNR
       loop
     endif
   enddo
     @ 7,42 say 'Record number .....'

*** Edit record number
```

```
                goto mRECNR
                row = 9
                for i=1 to 1024
                if row > 21 .or. "" = Fieldname(i)
                  row = 9
                  read
                  clear gets
                    @ 9,1 say space(79)
                    @10,1 say space(79)
                    @11,1 say space(79)
                    @12,1 say space(79)
                    @13,1 say space(79)
                    @14,1 say space(79)
                    @15,1 say space(79)
                    @16,1 say space(79)
                    @17,1 say space(79)
                    @18,1 say space(79)
                    @19,1 say space(79)
                    @20,1 say space(79)
                    @21,1 say space(79)
                endif
                if "" = Fieldname(i)
                  store 2000 to i
                  loop
                endif
                if type(Fieldname(i)) = "M"
                    @ row,1 say Fieldname(i)
                  set color to /w
                    @ row,12 say 'Memo'
                  set color to w
                else
                  store Fieldname(i) TO mFLD
                    @ row,1 say Fieldname(i)
                    @ row,12 get &mFLD
                endif
                do case
                  case type(Fieldname(i)) = "C"
                    if len(&mFLD) > 66
                      row = row + 1 + int(len(&mFLD)/66)
                    else
                      row = row + 1
                    endif
                  otherwise
                    row = row + 1
                    endcase
                    next i
                enddo
                close databases
                    @ 5,0 clear
                return
```

dAPPEND.PRG

```
        * Program Name ......... dAPPEND.prg
        * Description .......... Append routine for Clipper

        *** Set up screen

        set color to /w
          @ 4,21 say '              APPEND A DATABASE FILE              '
        set color to w
          @ 6,0,8,79 box frame2
          @22,0,24,79 box frame2
          @ 8,0  say chr(211)
          @ 8,1 say replicate(chr(196),78)
          @ 8,79 say chr(189)
```

```
    @22,0  say chr(214)
    @22,1 say replicate(chr(196),78)
    @22,79 say chr(183)
    @ 7,2  say 'Database file .....'
    @ 7,42 say 'Record number .....'

*** Set memvars

store space(10) to mFILENAME
store space(14) to mDBFNAME

*** Enter file name
do while .T.
  set color to w+
    @ 7,2  say 'Database file .....'
    @23,26 say '[ENTER] = return to Main Menu'
  set color to w
    @ 7,22 get mFILENAME picture '@!'
  read
    @23,26 say space(29)
  if mFILENAME = space(10)
    @ 5,0 clear
    return
  endif
  store mFILENAME+".DBF" to mDBFNAME
  if file('&mDBFNAME')
    exit
  else
    ? CHR(7)
    set color to w+*
      @23,35 say 'Not Found!'
    set color to w
      @ 4,79 say ''
    X=0
    do while X < Delay
      X=X+1
    enddo
      @23,35 say space(10)
    store space(10) to mFILENAME
    loop
  endif
enddo
  @ 7,2  say 'Database file .....'

*** Append blank record

use &mFILENAME
append blank
do while .T.
  set color to /w
    @ 7,62 say str(RECNO(),6)
  set color to w

*** Edit record number

  row = 9
  for i=1 to 1024
  if row > 21 .or. "" = Fieldname(i)
    row = 9
    read
    clear gets
      @ 9,1 say space(79)
      @10,1 say space(79)
      @11,1 say space(79)
      @12,1 say space(79)
      @13,1 say space(79)
```

174

```
                      @14,1 say space(79)
                      @15,1 say space(79)
                      @16,1 say space(79)
                      @17,1 say space(79)
                      @18,1 say space(79)
                      @19,1 say space(79)
                      @20,1 say space(79)
                      @21,1 say space(79)
              endif
              if "" = Fieldname(i)
                store 2000 to i
                exit
              endif
              if type(Fieldname(i)) = "M"
                  @ row,1 say Fieldname(i)
                set color to /w
                  @ row,12 say 'Memo'
                set color to w
              else
                store Fieldname(i) TO mFLD
                  @ row,1 say Fieldname(i)
                  @ row,12 get &mFLD
              endif
              do case
                case type(Fieldname(i)) = "C"
                  if len(&mFLD) > 66
                    row = row + 1 + int(len(&mFLD)/66)
                  else
                    row = row + 1
                  endif
                otherwise
                  row = row + 1
              endcase
              next i
          enddo
          close databases
            @ 5,0 clear
          return
```

Appendix C

Summary of Commands

Appendix C provides a summary with description of the commands that are used in this book.

Command Name	Description
?	Displays or prints an expression on the next line.
??	Displays or prints an expression on the current line.
@ *row,column*	Displays an expression at the row and column specified.
&&	Allows comments to be placed on the same line after a command.
!	Same as .NOT.
ACCEPT	Stores an entered expression in a memory variable (memvar).
APPEND	Appends (adds) a record to a database file.
APPEND BLANK	Appends (adds) a blank record to a database file.
CLEAR	Clears the display screen.
COPY FILE	Copies a file.
CREATE	Creates a structure-extended file.
CREATE FROM	Creates a database file with a file structure determined by the CREATE command.

Command Name	Description
DELETE	Marks a record for deletion.
DISPLAY	Displays records in a database file.
DO	Executes a named program or procedure.
DO CASE	Allows branching based on different case conditions.
DO WHILE	Executes program commands during a conditional loop.
EXIT	Escapes from a DO WHILE loop.
FIND	Searches for the first record in an indexed database file that meets a specified condition.
FOR . . . NEXT	Executes program commands during a conditional loop based on numeric increments or decrements.
FUNCTION	Identifies a user-defined function.
GET	Used with @ to display user-entered data.
GO/GOTO	Moves the database pointer to a specified record.
IF . . . ENDIF	Executes program commands based on a specified condition.
INDEX ON	Creates an index file based on selected sort criteria.
LOOP	Returns program execution to the previous DO WHILE command.
MENU TO	Waits for a user keypress during a Clipper menu.
PACK	Removes database records that have been marked for deletion.
PARAMETERS	Identifies characters that have been passed from a calling program.
PROMPT	Used with @ to display Clipper menu prompts and messages.
PUBLIC	Declares memory variables that are globally available within an application.
QUIT	Closes all files and exits to the DOS prompt.
READ	Allows user entry of data into an identified GET.
RECALL	Removes the DELETE marking of a record.
REINDEX	Rebuilds a database index file.
RELEASE	Erases specified memory variables.
REPLACE	Changes identified field content of a database file to that specified.
RESTORE SCREEN	Repaints the original screen display as

Command Name	Description
	previously specified with the SAVE SCREEN command.
RETURN	Terminates a program or procedure and returns control to the calling program.
SAVE SCREEN	Places the current display screen in memory for subsequent recall with the RESTORE SCREEN command.
SEEK	Searches for the first record in an indexed database file that meets a specified condition.
SELECT	Activates a specified work area (up to 10 are allowed in Clipper).
SET BELL	Turns the computer bell (beep) ON or OFF.
SET COLOR TO	Sets display color attributes to that specified.
SET CONFIRM	Requires the user to complete a GET by pressing the Return key (when set ON).
SET CONSOLE	Directs output to the display screen (when set ON).
SET DELETED	Causes records marked for deletion to be displayed and processed like other records (when set ON).
SET ESCAPE	Allows the ESC key to be used to suspend a program operation by pressing ALT-C (when set ON).
SET EXACT	Requires an exact match between specified characters (when set ON).
SET FILTER TO	Causes a database to display and process records only according to the selected filter criteria.
SET MESSAGE TO	Used in Clipper menus to identify the line where menu messages are displayed with the PROMPT command.
SET PRINT	Directs output to the printer (when set ON).
SET RELATION TO	Links two database files based on a specified common field or expression.
SKIP	Causes the database record pointer to go forward or backward the specified number of records.
STORE TO	Stores a specified expression into a memory variable.
USE	Opens a database in the specified work area.
WAIT " "	Suspends program operation until a key is pressed.

Appendix D

Summary of Functions

Appendix D provides a summary of the functions that are used in this book.

Function Name	Description
&	The macro substitution function.
BOF( )	Returns .T. when the beginning of the file is reached.
CHR( )	Returns the character conversion of a number.
CTOD	Returns the date equivalent of a character string.
DATE( )	Returns the current system date.
DELETED( )	Returns .T. if a record is marked for deletion.
DTOC	Returns the character equivalent of a date.
EMPTY( )	Returns .T. if a character string is blank, a date string is blank, a number is zero, or a logical expression is .F.
EOF( )	Returns .T. when the end of the file is reached.
FIELDNAME	Returns the specified field name.
FILE	Returns .T. if the specified file name exists.
FOUND( )	Returns .T. if the record being searched for exists.

Function Name	Description
INKEY( )	Returns the ASCII equivalent of a keypress.
ISPRINTER( )	Returns .T. if a printer is connected and online (EXTENDA).
RECCOUNT( )	Returns the number of records in a database.
RECNO( )	Returns the current record number.
REPLICATE	Repeats a specified character a specified number of times.
SPACE	Repeats a blank character a specified number of times.
STR	Returns the character equivalent of a number.
TRANSFORM	Returns the character equivalent of a character string or number in a specified format.
TRIM	Returns a character expression without the trailing blanks.
TYPE( )	Returns the data type of a variable.
VAL	Returns the numeric equivalent of a character expression.

Index

Edited by Marianne Krcma